PRAISE FOR BEING COACHED

"This book will have the same impact in the field of coaching as Lencioni did on the dysfunctions of the team. Deaton and Williams have translated the group coaching process into a fable that we can read, learn from, and enjoy."

—Katherine Ebner, Founder, The Nebo Company, Director of Georgetown University's Institute for Transformational Leadership

"The characters, management concerns and attitudes, and business situations are very comparable to the real world. The story setting and quick chapter format make it easy to absorb. As someone who has been coached, and who has experience on leadership teams with the typical team dysfunctions displayed here, this book showed me how coaching can help leaders help themselves. A typical leader might feel that they already have an action-oriented, overloaded management team, or that group coaching is too 'touchy-feely' and will come across as a sign of management weakness. The situations depicted in this book, however, show how group coaching breaks down walls and helps talented teams become even more high-performing. A wonderful and illuminating read!"

—Luke Wimer, EVP, Global Operations, MoneyGram International

"I love this book! I love the honesty, humor, and reality of the dialogue, the situations, the challenges, and the approach. I love the progression of the story—from start to ending. I love that this book positions group coaching for a leader—and will help leaders who are unsure what group coaching is see how it can benefit them. Of course, I love that the characters reveal their truths and that they, indeed, are the 'curers' of their team ills AND that the coach is simply the mirror and catalyst for conversation. A beautiful and powerful handbook for coaches, and the executive leaders they serve."

—Kristin Kaufman, PCC, CLC, Author of *Is This Seat Taken?*

"This book was an easy read, and it closely matches what really happens in organizations. Up-and-coming leaders who read *Being Coached* will know how they can use coaching."

—Ross Creasy, IT executive

"*Being Coached* is an engaging, realistic, and refreshing look inside the process of group and team coaching—a powerful tool for organizational change and personal growth. Whether you are a leader curious about the process, a coach wanting to know how to coach groups, or a human resource professional wondering how team coaching could work in your organization, this book is a rich resource that is easy to follow and enjoyable to read."

—Kelly Lewis, Sr. Leadership
Director, Luck Companies

"This book is very timely; many coaches have talked about group coaching, but there is very little written about the subject and I haven't found anyone who can explain it well. The style, relating a story of a (typically) dysfunctional leadership team and management, is engaging and thought provoking. I was immediately captured and couldn't wait to see what happened next. The coaching world will benefit greatly from a book that so clearly demonstrates how group and team coaching can benefit leadership teams and especially middle managers."

—Kathy Harman, CSC, MCC, Agile Team Coach and Author of *PRISM Teams*

"*Being Coached* is a totally unique book that fills a gap in the coaching world. As coaching has become more common, leaders, HR professionals, as well as coaches, can sometimes overlook the profound experience that occurs inside the mind and heart of the person being coached. Deaton and Williams have given us a glimpse of the transformational nature of the coaching process and made a significant contribution to the world of leadership development."

—David Emerald, author *Power of TED** and Donna Zajonc, MCC,
Director of Coaching and Practitioner Services, *Power of TED**

"What an intriguing book! Its story-telling style is reminiscent of Lencioni's *Five Dysfunctions of a Team*, yet unlike anything I have seen in the leadership coaching field. This book will enable readers to understand how team and group coaching open up possibilities and change the relationships that are the life's blood of all organizations. I appreciated the questions and essential points at the end to offer readers (whether HR professionals, leaders, or coaches) a deeper dive so they can easily pull out applications for their own work."

—Jean B. Gasen, PCC, PhD, Executive Director, Center for Corporate Education,
VCU School of Business Foundation

"In *Being Coached*, Deaton and Williams have done a great job of showing the distinctions between group and team coaching, driving home the value of both in an organization. The book's extremely realistic dialogue and examples made me feel like I was literally in the room during the conversations. Valuable book for leaders, coaches, and all whose work focuses on bringing out the best in their people!"

—Denise Kasper, MBA, SPHR, PCC, Executive Coach,
Financial Services Industry

"The field of team coaching is rapidly growing, and Ann Deaton and Holly Williams have brought a fresh perspective by providing engaging stories of what it feels like to be part of a team being coached."

—Professor Peter Hawkins, author of the best-selling *Leadership Team Coaching*

"If you're wondering whether investing in coaching will be worth the time and costs involved, read *Being Coached!* The authors paint a vivid picture of the purposes, processes, and lasting results of effective group coaching, answering the what's, why's and how's through an engaging narrative based on real teams."

—Jane A. G. Kise, EdD, author of *Unleashing the Positive Power of Differences*

"*Being Coached* portrays the challenges and dynamics of a group of senior leaders as they seek to hone their leadership skills. Drawing from their vast experience as coaches and leaders themselves, Ann Deaton and Holly Williams give us access to the interpersonal conversations and inner dialogues of vivid characters like those we meet in hallways and conference rooms every day. We follow these leaders from their initial skepticism of the coaching process, through their breakdowns and breakthroughs, and finally to success as they internalize their new suites of leadership behaviors. This book will be an asset to anyone who wants an honest picture of what it is like to be coached and what kinds of results can be expected if one is willing to do the work of being coached."

—Jonathan H. Ward, MSSM, PCC, Sr. Talent Management Consultant

"As a CEO of a rapidly growing company, I've learned that company culture is absolutely critical to success. Executive coaching—both individual and across a leadership team—helps define and then reinforce culture. *Being Coached* is a true-to-life story of team coaching. Not only did it remind me of my experiences as a CEO, but it also reinforced why team coaching has become a multiplier for our company's continued growth and success."

—Lynn Ann Casey, Chief Executive Officer, Arc Aspicio

"As the author of *Reality-Based Leadership*, I am always on the lookout for drama-diffusing tools—real tools that really work and that leaders will actually use. I was thrilled to find this book an incredible resource on group coaching—what an easy way to ditch the drama in teams, restore sanity to the workplace and develop leaders in the realities of limited resources! *Being Coached* presents a great breakthrough for maximizing the ROI on coaching. Authors Ann Deaton and Holly Williams take the development strategy of coaching, which traditionally focuses on changing the behavior of one, and show you how to bring it to the masses through group coaching. Groups conserve your energy while delivering exponential outcomes by changing the behaviors of many and the results for the organization. I am now using group coaching to develop my very own growth lab to create an arena to adopt, practice and apply Reality-Based Leadership principles in my clients' workplace."

—Cy Wakeman, HR Thought Leader and *New York Times* best-selling author
of *Reality-Based Leadership* and *Reality-Based Rules of the Workplace*

BEING COACHED

COACHED

GROUP AND TEAM COACHING FROM THE INSIDE

ANN V. DEATON & HOLLY WILLIAMS

MAGUS Group LLC, Broad Run, VA

Printed and bound in the United States of America
ISBN: 13: 978-0-615-97515-3
Library of Congress Control Number: 2014903552

(Being Coached: Group and Team Coaching from the Inside)

CONTENTS

PREFACE

At the core of *Being Coached: Group and Team Coaching from the Inside* are leaders in the midst of the daily demands of their work. The eight leaders in the group coaching program and the six senior leaders being coached as a team are the storytellers here—not the coach or the human resource professionals who sponsor coaching. We trust that you will enjoy and appreciate getting to know these leaders, and most likely see yourself in some of them.

Though several mentors suggested we choose just one audience for *Being Coached*, we've been aware of three audiences—leaders, coaches, and human resource professionals. We have written for the leader who is curious about what happens in team and group coaching. We have written for the coach who wants to know how group and team coaching work and how they might coach a group or a team. And we have written for the human resource professional who wants to understand how group and team coaching could work in their organization.

Much of the action in this book takes place outside of the group, team, and individual coaching sessions, as it does in real life. This reflects our belief that the true power of coaching lies in what takes place when the coach isn't there—that is, the process of change and development that happens inside each leader in the moment of choice while she or he is leading. Though the leaders in *Being Coached* each have their own authentic voices, none of the characters are based on leaders we have coached and any resemblance through name or deed is accidental and random.

As group and team coaches, our fundamental coaching assumption is that everyone wants to be a better leader. To that end, the foundation of both group and team coaching is developing leaders. In team coaching, the team must solve something together; each leader being his or her best self is critical to stepping up to the bigger game as a team. And when leaders from different teams are coached in a group, the community and collaboration that arises is a wonderful side effect as group members interact and support one another in their individual growth. Both group and team coaching help individuals to develop, and at the same time create a richer set of relationships that contributes to the organization thriving. You'll experience that here in the stories of these leaders.

Our own experience coaching has shown us that coaching at its best is wonderfully in the moment. It depends on co-creation and the energetic connection between leader and coach. To write a prescriptive book that tells coaches what to do in those moments would be limiting. Each reader will walk away from *Being Coached* with a different "aha." Some of you may realize how valuable it could be to be more transparent in your work. Others may come away with a tool that you'll apply immediately, or share with your team. We have included additional resources at the end of the book to support you as you apply lessons learned here.

We thank you for your interest in *Being Coached*, and we welcome your feedback.

Ann Deaton
ann@beingcoached.com

Holly Williams
holly@beingcoached.com

ACKNOWLEDGMENTS

I have such a deep sense of gratitude as I see this book finally complete and ready to be shared. There are so many to thank for their contributions. First and foremost, I have been inspired by the wisdom and commitment of the leaders I've coached. I want to acknowledge your many gifts. You teach me something new about leadership and courage every day.

I want to acknowledge my family. Judy and Nicholas, I appreciate your unending support as well as your lovely impatience to see *Being Coached* completed. Thank you to my siblings Kate, Jo, Tony, and Tim, always willing to listen, read, and critique what I've written. I appreciate my mom, whose love of unique words survives her, and my dad, the first book author in our family.

Thank you to my own coaches on the journey, especially Donna Zajonc, MCC, who trusted and challenged me to write my book. I know she is expecting at least one more from me. My friends and coach colleagues who've offered your support are many, and you will all know how grateful I am to you even as the limited space here keeps me from listing each of you.

This book wouldn't be in your hands now without Laura Maddox, Bethany Kelly, and Frank Steele, and your amazing array of talents. And, of course, thank you, Holly, for the invitation to write this book together and your willingness to learn with me along the way.

Ann V. Deaton, PhD, PCC

Oh, but there would be no book without Laura Maddox, whose witty, generous, and rigorous editing work helped us pull *Being Coached* into shape.

And thank you also to my family: My mother Alice who has written several books of poetry and fiction, my daughter Leah who writes wonderful fantasy fiction, and my daughter Arrien who is always curious and interested in "the book!"

Coach friends encouraged along the way: thank you to Dianne Falk, Erin Heiser, Jonathan Ward, Jennifer Whitcomb, Shari Jaegar, Barbara Braham, Lori Ermi, Karen Boskemper, Libby Graves, and many others who have listened, coached, and prodded (you know who you are) this book into being.

To Ann, the amazing coach who agreed to write this book with me!

And to the leaders and coaches who have inspired me—you are everywhere.

Holly Williams, MBA, PCC

PART 1

TECH ENVIRONMENTS GETS GROUP COACHING

1

IS COACHING THE ANSWER?

Patrick was anxious about his upcoming performance review, and that was unusual for him. As Director of Talent Management for Tech Environments, Patrick was beginning to realize that there was a lot he didn't know about developing the talent he had recruited. Ellen, TE's Chief People Officer, had informed Patrick last week in one of their regular meetings that she was expecting more of him. She had given him a pretty decent budget for leadership development and had suggested he start piloting some training classes right away.

Developing C-suite leaders was easy. These guys (and women, he reminded himself) were knowledgeable and experienced. A few of them had already worked with an executive coach to help them deal with the inevitable challenges, though Jack, their CEO, had resisted getting a coach thus far.

But middle managers were harder. Some of them weren't very experienced; others were overly confident and not so good at listening. A few didn't trust themselves to take risks and learn something new. Though the middle layer of managers clearly needed development, there was no way Patrick could justify executive coaches for each of them. And he knew he'd never find a training class that would work for every single leader. As far as he could tell from the variety of leadership problems they were having, everyone needed to get better at something different.

Enter Jordan, an executive coach Patrick had worked with over the years, at both his former company and Tech Environments. Patrick trusted Jordan, but he hadn't really thought to ask her about developing middle managers until a couple of days ago. Jordan had stopped by to say hello on a day when Patrick was feeling pretty desperate. One right after another, Marianne, Arthur, Alice, and Sheila, all decent managers, had ended up in his office with complaints and problems. Patrick was busy. He knew that they needed to develop as managers, and he didn't know how they were going to develop more leadership capacity. It certainly wasn't going to happen accidentally—nor would it happen if he only continued to give them advice, which they never seemed to take anyway.

After he explained his problem to Jordan, she offered a solution: pilot a leadership group coaching program. Patrick knew a little about the concept of group coaching but hadn't seen it work. Jordan had shared a couple of slides with evaluation data from past programs and a simple calendar of the schedule: six sessions of group coaching over five months for eight of their middle managers.

Group Coaching Calendar

	Week 1	Week 2	Week 3	Week 4	Week 5
January →			Initial 1-hr Individual Coaching	Pre-reading Homework	Pre-reading Homework
February →	1st 2-hr Group Coaching	Homework Peer Coaching	Homework Peer Coaching	2nd 2-hr Group Coaching	
March →	2nd 1-hr Individual Coaching	Homework Peer Coaching	3rd 2-hr Group Coaching	Homework Peer Coaching	
April →	Homework Peer Coaching	4th 2-hr Group Coaching	Homework Peer Coaching	Homework Peer Coaching	
May →	5th 2-hr Group Coaching	Homework Peer Coaching	Homework Peer Coaching	6th 2-hr Group Coaching	Final 1-hr Individual Coaching
June →		Evaluations			

○ **Three 1-hr Individual Coaching Sessions** with each leader, at beginning, midpoint, and end

● **Six 2-hr Group Coaching Sessions**, scheduled every 3 weeks

○ **Homework and Peer Coaching**, scheduled in between

In describing how group coaching worked, Jordan stressed that each manager would have his or her own leadership development goal, and that through individual, peer, and group coaching, every leader would develop in the way they needed over the five months of the program—mainly by being accountable for their own development.

When Jordan explained that group coaching would require homework, just like executive coaching, Patrick wondered out loud, "Are our middle managers going to be ready to make that commitment? They're pretty busy already."

"I have found with other clients that if the program is positioned correctly—a differential investment in high-potential managers who are seen as future leaders—then you will have no trouble gaining commitment for the program. But the selection process is important, and you may want to involve Jack, Ellen, and the rest of the senior leadership team in choosing which high-potential leaders you want in the first program."

"You mean stacking the deck?" asked Patrick.

"Not really, but you do want to select your top leaders so they can be role models for the rest of the company. If they are the leaders who consistently get results, in the most challenging roles, then they will probably be hungry for leadership development. Besides, many people have heard of coaching now, and it's a great perk for it to be offered to middle managers, not just senior leaders."

Patrick had decided to take the leap, and recommend leadership group coaching to Ellen and the senior leadership team.

Jordan said they could start within a couple of weeks, once the leaders had been chosen and the first executive coaching session had been set up, along with the rest of the schedule of group sessions.

He recommended Marianne, Sheila, and Arthur, and then he considered what other high-potential middle managers they might invest in. Kim would be a good recommendation, he thought, because she was new and in a really important role. Before he knew it, he had created a list of participants for the first leadership group coaching program at Tech Environments—a pilot program, he reminded himself, in case it didn't go well. He looked forward to making the case for group coaching with Ellen, and then the rest of the senior leadership team.

Soon, with all the free time he would have because managers would be talking to their new coach, Jordan, he would be able to get some other work accomplished too!

2
SHEILA WORRIES

Sheila was worried. What if her assessment[1] came back with some embarrassing information revealing her insecurities and flaws? Why had she ever agreed to be a part of this coaching program? She could have easily turned down the opportunity, given her new role as head of process improvement. The one thing that cheered her up a bit: the assessment only took about 20 minutes to complete, although some of the questions were kind of strange. She sighed when she remembered that her first meeting with the executive coach was coming up in a few minutes. *Hope that goes okay,* she thought to herself. *Here goes nothing.*

"Hi. You must be Sheila?" a woman with kind eyes and a soft voice asked as Sheila came into the room. She had a blue folder in front of her, and she got up to shut the door behind Sheila.

"Yes, I am. And you must be the coach, Jordan?"

Jordan nodded as they shook hands and both sat down, and Jordan began with her first question.

"Okay, tell me about yourself—from birth till now, or you can work backward if you want."

Sheila gulped and then asked, "You just want work stuff, right?"

"No, I'd like to hear everything—where you were born, how many brothers and sisters you have, what you liked in school, basically every-thing, at least the gist of it…"

Sheila took a deep breath and started. First she told Jordan about her parents coming to California, without any knowledge of English and without any money. Then it was about her mom, who had to work two jobs while raising Sheila and her younger brother. She recalled how her mom always said that Sheila would be the one to make her proud, to take care of her brother, and to do well in school. So Sheila did.

No matter how hard she worked or how much Sheila did, it wasn't enough. "Why isn't that A an A+? Why are you letting your little brother watch TV in the afternoons?" her mother would ask. Flash forward to now, and Sheila's 30-year-old brother is still watching TV in the afternoons while their mom works, and Sheila is an often-promoted midlevel manager in a big company, making great money but trying to figure out why she still hears her mom's angry voice buzzing around in her head when she hasn't returned all her emails, or the PowerPoint deck has a typo.

Jordan and Sheila sat in silence to digest everything, and Sheila felt a strange mixture of relief and embarrassment at having talked so much and about so many personal things.

"I appreciate your sharing that with me. It's helpful to have a sense of where you come from," said Jordan.

Then Jordan switched gears, "Did you see anything in the assessment you took that stood out?" she said, as she opened the blue folder and pulled out a data summary sheet.

"I see that according to this, I am hugely self-critical, which is affecting my self-confidence."

"And is that how you perceive yourself?"

"Totally, and I can't believe that this assessment nailed me."

"Would you like to work on that during this group coaching program?"

"Absolutely," replied Sheila.

3
CHARLES BEGINS

So here I am, sitting in a chair, me, Charles, realizing that I just told this perfect stranger, now my coach, how much I love ice hockey and how being at work just doesn't measure up anymore. Here's how it started…

We were talking about what I loved about college, and how great it was to play ice hockey and learn about psychology, and how excited I was to be part of a team when I first got here, and how much I used to love my job. That's right, used to love it. Now when I get up in the morning, as soon as I remember where and who I am, I get that feeling of dread, knowing that I have to go in and push and push and push all day, but still nothing happens and I'm not in control of anything.

It feels really weird to be bummed out *and* successful at the same time—I just got another promotion to Lead Program Manager, but I felt like saying no.

"Would you like to focus on that, Charles, in our group coaching program?" asked Jordan, the executive coach.

"You mean focus on how work isn't fun anymore and I really don't understand why?"

"I'm here to support your development agenda, Charles. How will we describe that goal in your coaching action plan?" she asked as she pushed the piece of paper over toward my side of the table.

"How about 'get back my enthusiasm for work?'" I asked.

"Okay, Charles."

I guess just talking about it and writing it down made a difference. I don't know, but somehow I felt lighter and cleaner. But that didn't last long. I remembered why I was down.

13

"Charles, when you get that feeling you described of being exhausted and unmotivated, where exactly do you feel that physically?" Jordan asked.

Boy, that was a great question… Hmmm.

"I get a heaviness in my chest first, and then I notice that my shoulders droop."

"It's good that you can be aware of that. Really, that's step one in the process," Jordan said.

We finished our session with a breathing exercise—it kind of took me back to the times when I worked on controlling my fear before a big game. I just took some slow regular breaths, noticing if I could keep the same rhythm with the in-and-out breath parts. Strange, but I did feel better. Maybe this coaching thing will work after all.

4

KIM HEARS ABOUT FEEDBACK

Wow, this seems like an inefficient way to explain things, I thought to myself as Jordan droned on about the purpose of the program, how often we would meet one-on-one and how we would have peer coaching, too. *Wonder why she doesn't just go through this at the beginning of the first group session, with a PowerPoint? Hope this won't be a total waste of my time.*

Then something she said actually caught my attention: "…and one of the things we will do is to gather some feedback about how you are showing up as a leader. You will select some people who know you and whose opinion you value, and you will develop a few targeted questions, schedule some time, and find out how they think you are doing, and how you could be an even more effective leader…"

Uh oh, I thought. I hate to get feedback, always have and always will. And I can't believe I will have to actually *ask* for it.

"You're looking alarmed. Is there a problem, Kim?"

"Well, you see, I have always hated getting feedback. It's hard for me to hear. I get defensive, and I shut down."

We sat in silence for a minute. Then she gently asked, "Is that something you would be interested in getting better at during the coaching program?"

I slowly replied, "I guess so."

"Are you sure?"

"Yes, I think I need to get better at it, or it will be hard to improve as a leader."

"Okay. I will help you with the questions, and your peer coach will, too. We won't do this right away; it will come later in the program, but I wanted to give you a heads-up. I'm glad you are willing to step forward into this."

I bet I won't really have a choice about getting the feedback, thought Kim. That's one thing she had noticed about being back at work after staying out so long with the kids—you always have to do some things you really don't want to do, even if you are a boss. No matter where you are in the food chain, there are going to be some things you just have to do.

5

ARTHUR EXPLORES

Arthur was running late for the group coaching meeting. "Why, oh why, did group coaching have to be scheduled today, of all days? We have a PowerPoint deck due to the CFO and I can't leave it in my team's hands. They need me to tell them what to do—even though we have done this deck before … several times before!"

Sure enough, everyone was already there except him, and they all looked at Arthur when he came in the door. "Sorry I'm late," he mumbled. Of course the only vacant seat was next to the coach, Jordan. *Figures*, Arthur thought to himself.

The conversation was already going about using a coaching approach with direct reports. That was the part Arthur didn't understand, really. It seemed to him that it would take a whole lot longer—maybe forever—to see if his team would come up with the answer. They always just looked at him and waited to be told. Sometimes he hated that. It took so much of his time to direct each of them, but they truly couldn't figure it out—he knew because he had tried before.

"What was your experience, Arthur, with the Lazy Coaching homework?" Jordan asked him.[2]

"Uh, it seemed like it took too long, and every time I asked, 'What else?' my direct report would look aggravated. Finally she just said, 'Why don't you tell me? I know you already have something in mind.'"

"That's how my conversation went the first time I tried it, too," Sheila broke in. "I am pretty on top of how I want something to be done. But I actually tried the Lazy Coaching approach in a group meeting of process owners, and it worked like magic. They got really excited about how they would solve the problem, and they came up with some great ideas. That's what I need in my job—a way to get process owners engaged."

Arthur listened and decided he would try again, when Kim broke in: "Here's what I did: I told my team that I was going to be trying out different approaches to leading and asked them to go along with me. That really helped—they want me to be a better leader, no doubt." Everyone laughed. Arthur thought he would have a hard time saying that—he expected a lot of himself and wasn't comfortable saying he didn't know how to do something.

This transition he was making—from a hotshot listened-to consultant at McKinsey to head of a work stream finance team—was proving to be harder than he thought it would be. Maybe he needed to have a different approach with his team here at Tech Environments. Maybe he wouldn't have to keep solving all the problems.

6
MARIANNE AND BEENA COMPARE NOTES

Marianne and Beena introduced themselves during the first group coaching exercise, which involved sitting with a peer coach and sharing something. During their conversation, they discovered that they had both worked at Tech Environments for ten years, that they were both married and had school-age boys, and that they were both ambitious and wanted a promotion.

But there the similarities ended. Marianne's problem—not an opportunity but a problem, she was sure of that—was her micromanaging boss, Patrick, who took credit for her work, went out of his way to be involved in the details of her team's work, and who seemed uncomfortable giving feedback or having a real conversation. Beena's manager was a dream: she had helped her get into her current role from which a promotion was expected, and she coached Beena frequently, especially before a major presentation. Marianne couldn't imagine that Beena had anything at all to work on to develop as a leader. It all seemed right there for her.

But when they shared their leadership development goals with each other, Beena confessed that she was troubled by second thoughts. She wondered whether or not she should go for the promotion, and how much more difficult her life might become. Everything worked right now, but just barely. How would she adjust to the additional demands? She wondered just how much harder it would be. When she expressed that fear to Marianne, Marianne muttered, "It couldn't be harder than doing your own work and having to justify it over and over like I have

19

to do." Beena was silent, because she hadn't experienced Patrick the way Marianne described him.

They agreed to coach each other on their development goals to see what would happen, using the thinking questions in David Rock's *Quiet Leadership* book.[3] Although they didn't achieve any breakthroughs, they did discover that they had both been thinking about their respective problems for a while, that solving them was a high priority, and that so far they had done nothing but worry about them. That was sobering!

Maybe there is something to this peer coaching after all, thought Beena. Marianne can help me with what she is really good at—being self-confident and able to have it all—and maybe I can coach her on coping with her manager.

7
RAJ SHOWS UP

Raj was thinking about how nervous he was and how he wished he could sound like everyone else. As he heard himself speaking, he could hear his voice getting softer and softer; he just wanted to go faster and faster to get it over with. Raj hated looking up and seeing others' puzzled looks and blank faces. He could already feel himself getting anxious about having to introduce himself to the group.

Before they started the introductions, Jordan asked everyone to take a minute to do a centering exercise—and there was even a neuroscience explanation behind it. Each person started observing his or her breath, and then started silently counting on the exhale. One, two, three, four, inhale … and starting over with one as they exhaled again. After repeating that three times, he felt calmer and more wide-awake. Those neuroscientists were getting practical now.

As Raj shared the origin of his name, he noted the interested looks around him. When it came time to reveal his development goal, he decided to take a risk and tell them about wanting to have more leadership presence and to be a better communicator. He explained his habit of speeding up to finish more quickly and to not have anyone challenge what he was sharing. Even though he understood it, Raj doubted that he could change it. He hadn't been able to yet.

After listening to his explanation, Sheila said, "You know, I used to do something like that—talking too fast, I mean, so I wouldn't be on the hot seat for long. It actually took longer because I had to repeat so much that people hadn't heard or understood. I was missing an opportunity to sway everyone's opinion when I talked."

Before Raj could respond, Arthur piped up, "Raj, your work is really important to our valuation program. I bet if others could hear and understand your ideas, they would want to make the changes you're recommending."

Then Jordan jumped in: "Raj, you can hear how engaged everyone is by your story. And I am curious about something. May I ask you a question?"

Raj nodded.

"Once we finished the centering exercise, you started speaking again and you seemed more relaxed and fluent than before. Did you feel that? What was different?"

Raj again nodded. "Actually, yes. It was easier to talk slowly and look at everyone. Then I started going inside my head, worrying, and things started speeding up. But the breathing seemed to help. That's something I could do—breathing and centering first and then speaking slowly, and trying to notice when I'm speeding up."

"We will support you in that practice during this program, Raj," Jordan said. "There will be lots of opportunities to share your opinions and feelings with everyone. And it's clear already that no one is shy about giving feedback." They all laughed.

8

ALICE CONFRONTS CHANGE

As she was reading an article about the brain's protective mechanisms, Alice thought back to a confrontation she'd had earlier in the week with one of her team members. They had been working on incorporating a major systems upgrade to a work stream that was also being outsourced, and the goal was to figure out how to sequence the communication to those who would be affected.

She realized that they had been going about it all wrong. They were trying to dictate how people should perceive the change and were arguing about their different versions of managing that.

But based on what she was reading in neuroscience, the better approach would be to let everyone make his or her own sense of the change, thereby overcoming the brain's natural resistance to others' ideas. It probably would be better to share the facts, explain the context for the change, then communicate more frequently, letting team members meet to discuss their reactions, and generate their own ideas on how best to implement and manage the change process.

Suddenly Alice had an insight. Maybe that was the best way for her and her colleagues to function as well. What if they could stop arguing over which was the best way to proceed and instead meet more frequently for shorter times and share how they felt about things, and what new ideas they were coming up with? What if she was able to step back from her strongly held beliefs about which way to proceed and let others come forward with their own ideas? Then as the team for leading change management processes for systems upgrades, they would be walking their talk by helping each other find their way through the change.

Excitedly, Alice reached for the notebook she was keeping as a requirement of the coaching program. She recorded her insights from the neuroscience article and how they applied to the changes she was trying to manage. How wonderful it would be to work on her leadership goal of better teamwork and also help further the big changes she, her colleagues, and their organization were going through!

She couldn't wait to share the article and discuss her new insights with the team.

9

JORDAN AND PATRICK MEET AGAIN

Jordan was happy. Reflecting on all of the first individual coaching meetings and the first group session, she was pleased. Most of the managers had seen themselves differently after reading and understanding the TAIS inventory results,[4] and for more than a few—Sheila and Charles quickly came to mind—the assessment showed them how they were getting in their own way. Charles's TAIS revealed his difficulty saying no, which was contributing to his being overwhelmed and lacking enthusiasm. Sheila's strong inner critic was driving her hard, affecting her both at work and home.

The others had different leadership development goals, Jordan realized. Both Arthur and Alice would probably find the shift to a Lazy Coaching approach helpful in their work with direct reports and colleagues. Marianne and Charles (again) would develop their skill in having difficult conversations through their work on saying no—and in Marianne's case it would be a powerful no to her overinvolved manager, Patrick. (Jordan reminded herself about the confidentiality of her role as a coach, and let go of her knowledge of Patrick as a supervisor so it wouldn't interfere with their conversation.)

Jordan thought that Raj's desire to work on leadership presence, Kim's worry about getting feedback, and Beena's proactive concern for work-life balance would lead them to discovering more about themselves as leaders. Once they understood their stories better, they would be freer to change them as scripts and create some new stories to live by.

All in all, it was a good group, with lots of diversity *and* commonality, and, for the most part, a willingness to explore how to develop as leaders and how to learn in a group. Patrick, Ellen, and the SLT had done a good job of selecting managers for the pilot group coaching program. Jordan was looking forward to meeting with Patrick and sharing some general themes about the first group session. She was thinking about how that conversation might go when the phone rang, and there he was.

"I hope you don't mind that I just picked up the phone and called you, Jordan," Patrick began. "I couldn't wait to hear how the first group session went, and what the development goals of the leaders are!"

"Not a problem at all. I was just thinking about the group and how they will be working together over the next four to five months. We had a great first session, with everyone there and participating fully. I was glad to see that they each had done their homework. As you know, Patrick, the way coaching works is that leaders take accountability for their own development and are willing to do the work even when the coach isn't there. Doing the initial readings, taking the TAIS assessment, and meeting with their peer coaches are good ways to see at the beginning how motivated they are. It also demonstrates that they understand that they are accountable for their development, not me!"

"If you could teach them that, you'd go a long way toward solving my issues with managing my own workload," Patrick blurted out. "I'm wondering if they think I like being involved in the details of their work. I can't make all the decisions about people."

Patrick continued by asking, "What are the development goals you are coaching?"

Jordan replied, "Here are some themes I am seeing," as she read from her notes:

- Wanting to develop greater leadership presence and clearer communication
- Needing to be able to handle conflict better and being able to say no
- Wanting to develop more confidence and quieting their inner critics
- Engaging colleagues and direct reports by asking more questions and using a coaching approach rather than being directive
- Seeking to maintain work-life balance
- And finally, getting better at dealing with a difficult manager.

"Hope that isn't me who's being described as a difficult manager. Marianne is in your coaching program."

"Your comment reminds me, Patrick, that we also discussed the confidentiality of coaching.[5] Nothing but general themes will be shared by me, and they are free to share anything, as long as they don't violate the confidentiality of their peer and group coaching agreements.

"The other thing I stressed is how important involving one's manager is in developing as a leader. One of their early assignments is to share their coaching action plans with their managers. I'm hoping those conversations will happen across the organization, and with you and Marianne too."

"Okay, I get it. I just couldn't help asking," Patrick said.

"No problem. Let's get back to development themes. What do you think based on what you heard?"

"They're great and not all that different from the development focus for many of our executives who receive coaching. I don't know why I find that surprising, but I do."

"Maybe it's because leaders drive their own development needs, and leaders tend to recognize similar opportunities. Fundamentally, coaching is self-discovery, so there are certain themes that will come up again and again, regardless of the level of the leader."

"Well, you are the expert!"

"Actually, they are!"

For Patrick, this call with Jordan was pretty typical. She often gave him something to think about, and often it was the last thing she said. He looked forward to his conversations with Marianne, though he had a sinking feeling that his tendency to micromanage was about to be called out. And he was also relieved to hear about the great start to the coaching program. Maybe the pilot would be really successful.

10
SHEILA TURNS A CORNER

Sheila walked into her office a few minutes ahead of her peer coaching session with Kim. *I can't believe that a couple of months ago this coaching group and Kim weren't even on my radar screen,* she thought. *I used to worry so much about my shortcomings that I felt like an impostor, sure on the outside but always doubting myself. Every once in a while now, I see my true self and what I actually bring to the company.*

Sheila had just finished jotting down her thoughts when Kim walked in. "Hey, Sheila!" Kim greeted her. "How'd it go with your mom this weekend?"

"Let's stick with work," Sheila responded glumly. "Visiting my mom this weekend threw me for a loop the way it always does. I really don't know how to deal with that woman!"

Kim surprised herself by staying quiet instead of jumping in.

Sheila continued, "I mean, just when I'm starting to hit my stride around here…" she gestured at her office and then trailed off. "I guess I just wish she could be on my side instead of always grilling me about what I'm doing and telling me what she thinks I should be doing. It makes me feel like I haven't accomplished anything."

"Sounds like it's getting under your skin all right," Kim responded. Then, remembering the Lazy Coaching model[6] they'd learned recently, she asked, "What have you thought of so far for dealing with her?"

"Well, I've thought about never seeing the woman again." They both laughed. "And I've thought about maybe taking a friend along so Mom would be on her good behavior," Sheila continued. "I really don't know what to do."

"What else have you thought of?" Kim was curious.

"Short of changing my identity, you mean?" Sheila chuckled, and then became serious. "I have actually kind of wondered if my mother is insecure

29

herself. I mean, she acts like she knows everything, but it seems like she's too concerned about my performance—like it reflects on her somehow."

"I know how *that* is," Kim said ruefully. "Being a mom opens you up for a lot of guilt. What else?"

"Well, I sometimes think I just need to get prepped for seeing her. You know, sort of how I get ready for a big presentation here. I'm so prepared that no matter what anyone asks me, I'm ready. Maybe I could do the same thing before I see my mom. But even saying that seems weird. I mean, I shouldn't be so bothered about it. She really does love me, no matter how she acts." The two women sat for a moment.

"So what will you do next?" Kim wondered.

"Wow, I just had an idea!" Sheila laughed. "It seems weird, but listen. I could just thank my mom for her input. Usually I feel like nothing I do is good enough for her, but I really don't have to take it so personally. I could just thank her for all her suggestions. And then I can take her advice … or leave it. That's what I do at work when I get a suggestion. I don't freak out; I just take it in and use it if it makes sense."

"That sounds awesome, Sheila. You almost look happy when you say that."

"I *am* kind of happy, Kim. It seems like a good way to deal with her. Between doing that and practicing a balanced assessment of my work— three things I did well in each meeting, and one thing I can improve—I think I might just start to feel as confident as I look sometimes. Thanks a bunch, Kim. I know you didn't think this simple stuff would really change anything, but it helped me today. You are great at this!"

"Let me know how it goes," Kim said as she headed out, thinking that while she was glad they had focused on Sheila, she wished there had been more time to get some conversation in about how nervous she was about getting feedback.

11
CHARLES STILL DOESN'T WANT TO BE AT WORK

All of this focus on leadership has me questioning everything, mused Charles, as he drove home one evening after most of the traffic had cleared. Even though he had promised himself (and his girlfriend) more balance in his life, here he was again, commuting home long after rush hour because he had stayed late on a project. There was so much to be done, and again, almost nothing under his control. How would he ever fix that?

One thing he had been noticing, though, was that tight feeling in his chest and his drooping shoulders. It seemed to him that he was pretty much always feeling that way at work now. Everyone kept asking him for help, and everything was taking so much longer to get done. Wonder when that feeling of overwhelm and resignation would ever lift?

Suddenly Charles remembered the Thinking Path[7] model they talked about in the group coaching program. How did that go? Oh, yes: how you are thinking will create feelings, which then drive behavior, which leads to results. He remembered that Jordan also said that the way to use the model is to notice when one feels bad. Well, this sure was one of those times!

So what *was* he thinking about? Well, for starters he was overwhelmed, and he would never be able to complete everything that everyone was asking of him. Just thinking that thought made him feel exhausted and sad. Remembering what went on earlier that day, he realized that when he felt exhausted and sad, he could feel himself slow down and become more distracted and begin to lose his confidence. The result of all that was missed deadlines and even more work and rework.

Thinking Path

Results

Actions

Feelings

Thinking

How could he think himself out of that?

All he could do now was keep driving home, promising himself that he would jot down what he discovered in his notebook—maybe documenting his current thinking path would at least be a start. He remembered that he had a peer coaching meeting with Arthur later in the week, so maybe that would be something to work on then. Oh yes, and one more thing he remembered: that maybe simply breathing deeply and sitting up straight with his shoulders back would help him feel calmer and more confident. Even right now, driving home, Charles could feel himself relax. He voice-dialed his girlfriend and offered, "Hey, I'm later than I wanted to be tonight. Can I grab take-out for us on the way home? I want to hear about your day."

Later that evening, Charles realized he had changed his mood and his evening just by focusing on what he wanted—a relaxing evening with his girlfriend—instead of everything that was wrong. Maybe things were more in his control than he realized.

12
KIM STRUGGLES WITH FEEDBACK

K im walked into her office, deep in thought. She had expected that her peer coaching with Sheila would be valuable to both of them, and she guessed it had been. She wanted to be a better listener, but that's not all she wanted.

Pulling up her email, Kim noticed a message from Patrick:

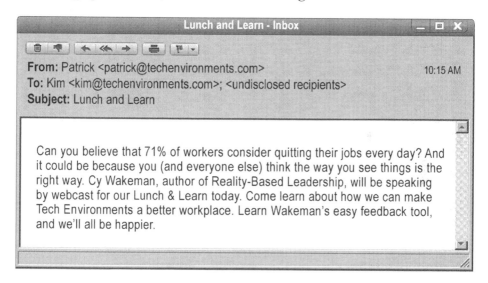

Wow, Patrick is really stepping it up a notch, Kim thought. *I've heard of Cy Wakeman, and I was just going to eat lunch at my desk.*[8,9] *I'll head on down instead. Feedback is my development area and maybe I will learn something.*

Fifteen minutes later, Kim was sitting in the large conference room with about thirty other managers. She spied Marianne and went over to join her.

"How's it going?" Marianne whispered. "I'm surprised to see you here. I, of course, *had* to come. This is Patrick's baby, and there's no way I could miss it."

Kim nodded and she opened her lunch, "I'm glad he reminded us," Kim said. "I was out most of last week, and I've just been catching up on everything. I didn't have this on my schedule."

The women became quiet as the webinar began.

From the beginning, Kim was riveted by the presentation. On the big screen, Wakeman was sharing stories about drama at work. "Lack of feedback is almost always at the root of organizational problems," Wakeman insisted. "How many of you are good at giving feedback?" Kim looked around her as only a third of the hands were raised. "How many of you like to receive feedback?" Half of those hands went down.

"Hmmm. Guess I'm not the only one who has trouble listening to feedback," Kim said to Marianne after the lunch. "I wonder if you have a couple of minutes to help me figure out how to give some feedback? I believe if I can give it more easily, I will be better at receiving it." Marianne agreed.

A few minutes later, the two women waved goodbye, and Kim headed back to her office. She quickly IM'ed her peer coach, Sheila:

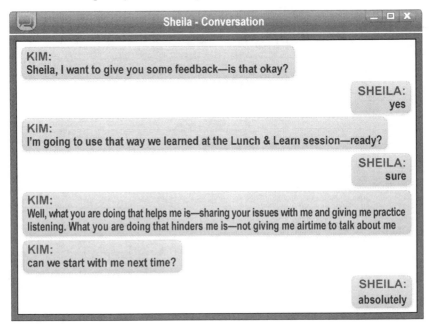

13
ARTHUR KNOWS HE'LL NEVER GET IT

"I wish this were working for me," Arthur complained to Jordan in a phone call. He had decided to reach out to the coach so he wouldn't embarrass himself in front of everyone else in the group. He knew he was way behind the others, and he was worried. But now Arthur was wondering if it was a mistake to call Jordan. Would she think he was completely clueless and drop him from the group? How disappointed would Patrick be that one of his so-called "high potentials" had flunked out of group coaching?

Jordan's warm voice brought him back to the here and now. "What have you tried so far?"

"That's why I'm calling you. I think I've tried everything. One week I told my team I wasn't going to solve everything anymore; I was going to trust them more. That didn't work, so the next week I tried the coaching thing we talked about—you know, 'What have you tried? What else? What else? What's next?'"

"Yes, I know the Lazy Coaching model," Jordan chuckled. "How did that work for you?"

"Not well," Arthur continued to gripe. "We are all busy all the time, so when I ask questions instead of telling people what to do, it just slows us down. I get frustrated, and everyone else does, too."

Jordan persisted, "What else?"

"You know, I really think I've given this a fair shot," Arthur insisted. "Can you just let me off the hook on coaching my team and move on to other things?"

"Sure, Arthur, we could absolutely do that if you want to give up. I'm just surprised. You seem so committed, so motivated to keep getting better and keep moving up at Tech Environments. And you are the one who chose this goal so you could transition from your consultant position to your new supervisor role. It's your call. Are you thinking you'd like to opt out of the group coaching altogether? I'm sure Patrick would understand based on your workload."

Surprised she would let him go that easily, Arthur didn't know whether to feel hurt or relieved. He decided he'd choose to be persistent instead. "Well," he said finally, "you are right that I never give up on anything. That's not my style. This is honestly the hardest thing I've ever had to do on the job, and I just feel like I'm not getting anywhere. I'm letting my team down. But you said something in the last coaching group that kind of grabbed me. You said it takes a courageous person to ask for help. That actually gave me an idea. I'm not sure if it makes any sense, but let me run it by you. What do you think about me asking my team to help me? I mean, that way, maybe if I am really screwing up, or everyone is frustrated, I can just ask *them* to help *me* out. I've told them some of the things I've learned in the group, so I think they know I'm working on my leadership. What do you think?"

"I think you might just have solved your own problem, Arthur. What do you think?"

"I'm going to give it a try. I'll let you know how it turns out." As he hung up the phone, Arthur felt a lot more confident than he had when they'd started. Maybe he could do this after all.

14

MARIANNE GETS IRRITATED AT PATRICK

Marianne was fuming as she walked back to her office. "I don't have time to do the work *and* meet constantly to update Patrick. He's my manager, I know, but why does he have to micromanage me? Why can't he trust me to manage my work?"

She didn't trust herself to have the conversation with Patrick because she was sure she would mishandle it, but she did pull up her calendar to see when her next conversation was scheduled with her peer coach, Beena. Perfect—this afternoon at 2:00!

Beena was great at just listening as Marianne shared with her the latest incident. Finally, when the story was over and Marianne had stopped to take a breath, Beena said, "Well, I just caught myself getting ready to give you advice, and it wasn't pretty! Instead, let me ask you, 'What are you thinking now?'"

Marianne reflected. "I'm not sure. I know I need to have a conversation with Patrick, but I don't trust myself to have it without getting mad."

"What else?" asked Beena.

"I need some help figuring out what to say and how to say it."

"What are you going to do?"

Marianne responded quickly, "I'm going to start reading ahead on the next book—*Fierce Conversations*, I think is the name of it."[10]

Suddenly she realized that Beena had been using the Lazy Coaching model from the group coaching homework, and she laughed out loud. "Are you getting brownie points for doing your homework, you lazy coach, you?"

"Well, it's working, isn't it?" asked Beena. "You know what you're going to do next, right?"

Marianne thought for a minute. Yes, she knew she had to confront Patrick and do it in a way that he could hear her and not get defensive or angry himself. That book on having tough conversations had better be good.

15
BEENA HAS A BREAKDOWN

Beena was in the middle of a breakdown. It all started with her husband's unplanned trip to India to see his dying father. The heart attack had been sudden, and his father wasn't expected to live. Beena's husband Eli had left that morning in a rush to make his flight.

Beena depended on Eli to be the one to manage things at home while he was finishing up his master's degree. The twins were at that impossible age—too old for a nanny and too young to be at school full-time. That left a patched-together pattern of preschool and babysitters and Eli, who could always work his school schedule around her long days at the office. Now she had all of the arrangements to handle along with her own scheduled business trip later in the week.

There is no way I can do this, thought Beena. *How can I manage this and even more responsibility at work? I am already feeling pulled apart by longing for my boys even though I know they are being well cared for. Now what?*

Her manager at work had asked her to step forward into a big new project. Beena was excited about the cross-functional team she would lead, but nervous about their willingness to follow her. One way she thought she could ensure that would be to always be available and to work harder than everyone else. Now that was not an option. She didn't know any other way to get the project delivered.

Luckily she had a coaching call scheduled with Jordan later that morning. If she could just get the children settled, she could share her woes with her coach.

Jordan's soft voice came through loud and clear: "Tell me what's going on."

Beena could hardly get the words out fast enough. As she described her current predicament, she could feel her chest tighten and her throat close.

39

Suddenly she stopped talking and started breathing, three counts in and five counts out for the exhale. After about half a minute, Jordan asked: "So what's occurring to you now, Beena?"

"That I am just making myself even crazier worrying about everything. But what I really want to know is this: how will I be able to deliver the project if I can't always be there with them?"

"Okay," said Jordan, "let's talk about this. The project leaders you admire, those who you willingly followed, what were they like?"

"Smart, funny, calm, focused, generous, willing to step back and let us lead…" Slowly Beena's voice trailed off as she realized what she was saying. "Oh, wow, that's just the opposite of being there every minute and hovering over everyone.

"Maybe I can do this…"

16
RAJ GETS THE NEUROSCIENCE BUG

Raj seemed to be sitting up straighter as they checked in for their next group coaching session. When his turn came around, he smiled at everyone, took a deep breath, cleared his throat, and announced, "I volunteered to be the master of ceremonies at our upcoming annual awards dinner. No one else wanted to do it, so I said I would."

Even his coaching partner Alice was surprised. "Wow, what got into you?" she asked.

"Actually, my manager did," Raj said. "She is in NSA, the National Speakers Association.[11] So when I told her my development goal is better communication and leadership presence in groups, she told me to get more practice in front of people, any kind of practice."

"When you take a leap, you really take a leap," Kim noted. "And you aren't even talking fast today. What's your secret?"

"Well, it really *is* my manager," Raj laughed, "though she doesn't quite understand why her advice was so good. She doesn't know the neuroscience like I am starting to. After our last group session, I finished reading David Rock's *Quiet Leadership* book."[12]

A couple of people rolled their eyes, vaguely remembering skimming the book. Neuroscience wasn't for everyone, and some weren't convinced about the explanations of behavior.

Raj ignored them and continued, "Anyway, I really liked Rock's idea that we can't necessarily change the way we are wired, but we *can* create new wiring and new habits. So when my manager told me to get more practice,

41

I realized she was saying the same thing—give myself some opportunities to lay down some new neural tracks, and I won't keep stumbling around when I speak."

"That's all good," said Kim, "except why would you be any better just because you do it more? You've been talking your entire career, and it's still been hard for you to do it well!"

"Whoa, gentle with my peer coach, Kim! You certainly *are* getting more comfortable with feedback," Alice jumped to Raj's defense.

"No, no. It's fine, Alice. Kim is actually right. Just speaking more wouldn't change anything in my brain's wiring unless I was speaking differently. That's where TED Talks came in."

"TED Talks?" Jordan asked.

"Yes," said Raj, "TED Talks. I love TED Talks. You all should watch them sometime. Anyway, I got curious about how my brain and my body connect, so I searched with the keyword 'body' on TED Talks and found this cool talk by a psychologist, Amy Cuddy, about how changing your body position can change your mind.[13] Even if you aren't really confident, there are ways you can stand and postures you can get in that actually make you feel more confident. If you change your body, it changes your mind. Then I started watching YouTube videos on the Alexander Technique, which is all about body awareness during movement.[14] I really want to develop more self-awareness about my body so it can help me instead of betraying me."

It was the longest and loudest anyone in the group had ever heard Raj talk. Kim finally said what they all were thinking, "Maybe it wasn't such a leap after all, Raj. Sounds like you did your research and you are really onto something. I'm impressed."

Looking around, Raj realized everyone had been mesmerized by his story. A great start on his leadership goal, he thought proudly.

17
ALICE SETS AN INTENTION

Well, that was a bust, Alice thought to herself. Instead of getting everyone to agree to her new change model, everyone reacted the way they almost always did—pushing back and arguing.

It seems like I just can't get along with people, she thought. *It's almost like I can't win for losing. I'm going to read some more about the brain. I thought I had a better clue about how to approach them without getting resistance. Maybe there is something I am not getting here.*

She picked up *Quiet Leadership* again, and turned randomly to a page and started reading.[15] It was the section on letting others come to their own insights, and why the brain fights ideas from others. Maybe she had been trying too hard. Maybe there was another way.

Alice's next team meeting was in a few hours. She set an intention, just like her coach Jordan had suggested, about how she wanted to show up. She visualized exactly what she wanted to happen, as well as her actions throughout the meeting. She planned to sit back, to actually lean back, and to open herself completely to everyone else's ideas. No matter what ideas came to Alice, she was determined to listen, not spout off. Remembering that she had tried that before, and how nervous it made everyone, she decided this time to tell the group what she was doing. And why. That way they wouldn't be distracted, wondering why she was silent. Maybe they could just forget she was there!

A few hours later Alice walked into the team meeting. They were in the habit of doing a quick check-in with each other at the start, and Alice shared her plan. Everyone looked carefully at her to see if she was for real. Then several people nodded, and everyone seemed pretty relaxed, even Bill, her nemesis, who argued with her about every single thing.

Soon the first disagreement surfaced. They had been arguing for weeks about when to introduce the change management process for the system users. Some people thought it needed to deploy prior to the system release, and others argued that it would slow production and get the users unnecessarily upset. This was one debate that Alice didn't actually have a strong opinion about. So it was a little easier to listen to each side. And in some inexplicably strange way, Alice's intentional listening seemed to create spaciousness in the conversation. *Maybe listening does beget listening*, she thought. Suddenly, Bill asked: "Alice, what do you think?"

This, in and of itself, was shocking. Alice couldn't remember Bill ever asking her for her opinion. Come to think of it, she had never asked Bill his opinion. She remembered a suggestion from her reading, so she used it: "I think there is merit to both sides—what do you think?" Before he answered, Bill shot her an appreciative look. Soon the group discussion was off and running again. And Alice felt great. She had followed her intention and it had worked. And she had something to share with her peer coach and in the next group coaching session!

18

PATRICK AND JORDAN RECONNECT

"Hard to believe we're halfway through the coaching program," Patrick mused. He had a check-in with Jordan in a few minutes, and he was looking over his notes so he would be familiar with the group coaching design. One of his associates, Marianne, was in the group coaching program, but she had thus far avoided talking to him about what she was learning. In fact, she was avoiding him most of the time now. *Hmmm, what was that about?*

There was a knock at his office door, and Jordan peeked around the corner. "You have time for me?"

"Of course, come in. How is it going?"

Jordan threw the question back at him: "What are you hearing?"

"Well, Marianne isn't speaking to me—what's that about?"

"Have you asked her?"

"No, but I will."

"What else are you hearing?" asked Jordan.

"Actually, not much from the participants, but I got some good feedback recently about Alice from her client. Apparently she is listening more and bossing the change management team around less, which makes her business partner happier. I also heard something about Charles seeming to be less overwhelmed."

Jordan said, "I think that's the best kind of feedback, what you are hearing from the leaders and others around them."

"How do *you* think it's going, Jordan?"

"I love how everyone is working together in our group coaching sessions, and I think the peer coaching is working great, too. So far, everyone is doing most of the reading and practicing between the sessions. And that is when coaching really happens: when the coach isn't there!

"And so I am pleased," said Jordan. "Could you keep listening for feedback? That's how we will know if we are truly developing leaders."

Patrick agreed to do that. He also listened and took notes while Jordan explained the next key program assignment: each leader would ask three or four leaders they admired, and who knew them, for feedback on their leadership in a two-way conversation. The questions were to be designed by the participants, and the conversation was to be scheduled in person during the final third of the group coaching program. The leadership feedback they received would inform the coaching development plan each leader would leave the program with, after the final executive coaching session.

Feedback assignment:

- 3–5 leaders (they admire, know them well)
- Questions created in group
- Each participant asks leaders for feedback during 1–1
- During the final third of the group coaching program
- Helps with development plan each leaves the program with

Patrick was impressed. It would be great for leaders this early in their careers to get comfortable asking for feedback and having leadership conversations with more senior people. *It will be interesting to see who they choose,* he thought, just as Jordan was saying, "I suggested they pick leaders who they admire—hopefully there are enough to go around in Tech Environments!"

Patrick thought to himself, *I want to be chosen to give feedback. I hope I am. But first, I'd better check in with Marianne and get some feedback.*

19
GROUP COACHING SESSION

Jordan glanced at her watch and wondered where Arthur was. Well, she was happy to see that most of the group was either on time or early. By now, everyone knew that the group coaching session would start on time no matter how many (or how few) were there.

Jordan asked if anyone could suggest a centering exercise to start. "Oh, I know," said Sheila. "Let's do a one-word check-in, followed by a 'what's *really* been happening over the past three weeks.'"

Everyone agreed, and Charles went first:

"*Shocked!*" he exclaimed. "That's my one word. Even though I've been hoping I could get a handle on my workload, I've been surprised, astonished really, by how getting a handle on my attitude makes a difference even when the demands are still just as heavy."

Alice followed with her word: *lean-back*. They all laughed at Alice's inability to use just one word. "It's a hyphenated word!" she joked. Then more seriously, "I had this great experience with my team, and it was all about me leaning back. I let them know my intention to listen and observe at the start of our team meeting, and I followed through."

"My word is *challenged*," Kim offered. "I'm really trying to give and accept feedback, but so far I'm not faring too well on the receiving end. It's harder than I thought. Getting ongoing, everyday, regular feedback is something you have to ask for, and I am really stuck on the part about asking."

"*Self*," said Raj. "You all are trying to listen to others. I'm trying to learn to listen to my self so I can get out of my own way."

"The word is *courage* for me," Marianne spoke softly. "I've got to get up courage to talk to Patrick, and soon! He's asked me three times already about my development goal."

"My word is *noticing*," Sheila chimed in. "I'm trying to notice the actual words I am saying to myself, rather than pushing them away because they are so harsh. I am finding that when I *notice*, I can change the words and coach myself rather than beat myself up."[16]

Beena was the last leader to share: "*Balance*," she stated unequivocally. Then abruptly she asked what everyone had been thinking, "Where's Arthur?"

They all shrugged and looked at Arthur's peer coaching partner, Charles. "I don't know either," he offered uncertainly. "I do know he's been having a tough time with his team, but I don't really want to say more than that. It was said in confidence."

Jordan supported Charles: "Yes, that was one of the agreements we all set for your peer coaching."

"Okay, but what about Arthur?" Beena persisted. Turning to Charles, she asked, "Will you check in on him for us?"

"Absolutely. I'm curious myself," Charles agreed.

Jordan nodded. "Thank you, Charles, and thanks for the check-in suggestion, Sheila. We've already started talking about some of the conversations you all have been having and are going to have. A great resource for this is one of the books on our list: Susan Scott's *Fierce Conversations*. Anyone taken a look at it yet?"

"I did," Marianne revealed. "The name *Fierce Conversations* seemed a little too aggressive for me until I read the first chapter and found out that 'fierce' just means robust, powerful, or intense.[17] That pretty much captures the conversation I need to have with Patrick. The book has already helped me: it's about how we get to where we are in our relationships 'one conversation at a time.'[18] And if we are in a bad relationship, we have gotten there one *failed* conversation at a time … in my case, it's a conversation I've altogether failed to have, with Patrick."[19]

Raj spoke up next, "I started reading it, too, and I really like the questions the author asks. I told you all that I am nervous when I speak, so I asked myself, 'When am I *not* nervous?' That has helped me to get a handle on what's happening when I'm communicating well."

"I love how you are applying the resources to your own development goals!" Jordan said, praising them.

In the glow that followed this compliment, she continued. "You'll get to go deeper into your awareness of yourself as a leader in our next assignment. You will have a chance to get feedback on your individual leadership brand, on how you are showing up now as a leader." She explained that they would be requesting feedback from three or four leaders who they admired. The discussion moved around the table as they explored who they would choose, what type of questions they would ask, and what it would be like to take on something like this. Some shared their nervousness about asking for feedback, though Beena and Raj seemed more excited than nervous.

Raj blurted out, "I'm going to start the conversation by asking, 'What leadership qualities do you admire?' Then, 'How do I stack up?'"

"That's a good one," Beena said. "I think I'll also ask, 'When have you seen me at my best?' And maybe, 'What trips me up?' I don't think we have to ask a ton of questions to get a ton of information."

"Sounds like you have a good start," affirmed Jordan. "Be sure to ask your peer coach for help if you get stuck. This is really one of the most powerful aspects of our coaching if you are willing to take the risk: asking for feedback and listening to what you hear. It will all be valuable, even if you disagree with it."

"To feedback!" Kim exclaimed wryly, as the group session ended.

ARTHUR APOLOGIZES

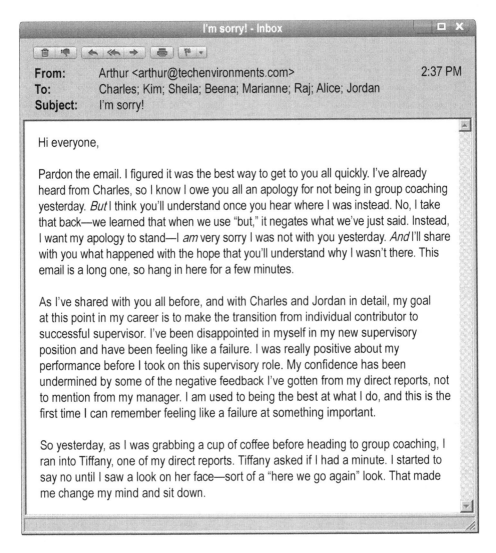

20

I'm sorry! - Inbox   ☐ X

From:	Arthur <arthur@techenvironments.com>
To:	Charles; Kim; Sheila; Beena; Marianne; Raj; Alice; Jordan
Subject:	I'm sorry!

2:37 PM

Hi everyone,

Pardon the email. I figured it was the best way to get to you all quickly. I've already heard from Charles, so I know I owe you all an apology for not being in group coaching yesterday. *But* I think you'll understand once you hear where I was instead. No, I take that back—we learned that when we use "but," it negates what we've just said. Instead, I want my apology to stand—I *am* very sorry I was not with you yesterday. *And* I'll share with you what happened with the hope that you'll understand why I wasn't there. This email is a long one, so hang in here for a few minutes.

As I've shared with you all before, and with Charles and Jordan in detail, my goal at this point in my career is to make the transition from individual contributor to successful supervisor. I've been disappointed in myself in my new supervisory position and have been feeling like a failure. I was really positive about my performance before I took on this supervisory role. My confidence has been undermined by some of the negative feedback I've gotten from my direct reports, not to mention from my manager. I am used to being the best at what I do, and this is the first time I can remember feeling like a failure at something important.

So yesterday, as I was grabbing a cup of coffee before heading to group coaching, I ran into Tiffany, one of my direct reports. Tiffany asked if I had a minute. I started to say no until I saw a look on her face—sort of a "here we go again" look. That made me change my mind and sit down.

I'm glad I did. Tiffany started by telling me she'd been thinking of applying for a different role in the company, something in another department. She shared how hard it had been for her to adapt to me as her supervisor, how much things had changed since I had come on board, and that she wondered if it would ever feel good to come to work again. Tiffany was close to tears, and we talked for over 45 minutes.

What she said was hard to hear. I won't share everything we talked about. What I will tell you is that I was able to own up to how bad I've been feeling since I was promoted. Just so you will know this—but please don't share it around—I have had some personal issues that I am dealing with. I know, I know, it is hard for me to share things like this, but my dad is having some health problems and my girlfriend just ditched me for someone else.

Anyway, I told her that I feel incompetent sometimes, and that I miss my old role where I was the expert. I told her how much I want to be a good supervisor, and how my manager and you all are helping me to learn how. And I asked for her help in getting better. We actually ended up laughing a couple of times when we talked about all the things that have gone wrong since I took over. What a bunch of misunderstandings and false starts. The bottom line is that Tiffany agreed to work with me in learning how to be a better leader of the team.

I trust you'll understand that this unexpected gift of a conversation over coffee felt like the most important thing I could be doing yesterday morning, even if it did mean missing group coaching.

Charles is going to catch me up on what you talked about together. I've already started reading *Fierce Conversations* and can see a lot of great applications for my team. Check out chapter 3—"Be Here, Prepared to Be Nowhere Else"—and you'll have an even better understanding of what happened to me yesterday![20]

Thanks for your support. It's partly because you all have been open with me that I knew how to be vulnerable and humble with Tiffany. That's new to me, and I think it could be an important part of being a good supervisor.

All my best,
Arthur

21

CHARLES TURNS A CORNER

Almost daily, someone commented on how happy Charles seemed. And they all wanted to play the guessing game: You're getting married? You broke up? You got a new client? Just back from vacation? He grinned and said no to every question, because the real reason was sort of hard to explain.

Charles had just decided to shift his thinking about work—from always thinking about being overworked and stressed out, to thinking positively about all of the areas where he had an impact and could contribute. Somehow, thinking that made him feel hopeful and energetic and not so stressed. Away from that place of darkness, Charles was able to get more work done and to be more encouraging of his project team members. Everything just seemed easier now.

Even his customer noticed. Charles had been assigned "The Worst Customer Ever," according to office lore. Ed was his name, and he was cranky, mean, and pretty much impossible to please. Before his epiphany, Charles had adopted a constrained "please don't kick me again" approach that seemed to spur Ed on to even more fury. Charles figured he should shift his attitude with Ed. Instead of thinking Ed was impossible and hateful, he replaced those thoughts with thinking that Ed had exacting standards and a real sense of what *his* customer, the federal government, might actually want. He started anticipating Ed's needs and asking questions of Ed to draw out how he was thinking. Charles was feeling more confident and capable, and, wonder of wonders, Ed started responding to him differently, too.

Next thing he knew, the big boss of the company was knocking on his door. Nervously, Charles got up to let him in, thinking, *Uh oh, this cannot be good news.*

Jack asked to come in, and he spent the next few minutes trying to joke around, which made Charles even more nervous. He had to give him some credit, though: he remembered Charles's long commute and the fact that he lived with his girlfriend.

Finally Jack came to the point: "I had a meeting with your client Ed's senior leadership team, and I never expected to hear this. In a project update, Ed shared with them how pleased he was with our work and what a difference it is having you lead our team."

In the silence that followed, all Charles could do was grin, his nervousness gone.

Jack cleared his throat and asked, "What did you do? We all want to do it, whatever it is."

"I just started thinking about things differently."

Jack looked confused, then smiled in a perplexed kind of way. After another long pause, he said, "Well, keep up the good work, Charles."

Charles couldn't stop grinning as the CEO stepped out of his office.

22

KIM'S COINCIDENCE

Kim was thinking so hard about the feedback assignment that she wasn't paying attention to where she was going, and almost bumped into Donna in front of the cafeteria. Kim knew Donna because they had started at Tech Environments on the same day and bonded at the orientation class held that first week.

Donna had a big job at Tech Environments—a C-level title having to do with marketing. She had sought out Kim to be on an upcoming special project on revenue analysis, and she always stopped for a conversation when they saw each other. This time she asked, "Going in or out? Would you like to have lunch? I'd love to hear what you are up to."

Kim happily agreed, thinking that this might be a good time to ask Donna to set up a meeting on the feedback assignment. Donna was really interested in Kim's description of the group and peer coaching, and she said she would be happy to help out. "Why don't we do this right now?" Donna asked. "I'd be glad to share what I've observed about how you show up as a leader."

As Donna said this, she noticed how uncomfortable Kim was getting. "Is this hard for you?" she asked gently. "Very hard," said Kim. "I really don't like the attention, and it's hard for me to even listen when people give me their impressions of me. I know I need to get better about getting feedback, and giving it too, but it still feels really awkward. When people look at me I am sure they notice how different I am from the rest of the people here at my level—I'm at least ten years older because I stayed home with my kids. I don't like people to notice that difference."

Kim stopped speaking abruptly when she realized that she was sharing this with Donna, who may have had her own issues about looking different since she was the only African American at the senior level, and a woman, too.

"Talk about awkward…" Kim's voice trailed off, and suddenly they were both laughing.

"It really *is* funny," said Donna, "how much we worry about these things and maybe nobody else does. I certainly had not picked up that you were self-conscious about anything. What I see is someone who is always ready to step forward, who leads through example by asking questions and seeking answers, and who demonstrates lots of empathy and encouragement of other team members' growth and development."

"Really?" asked Kim.

"Really," said Donna.

Kim was delighted to hear that Donna could so easily speak to the areas where Kim had shown up well as a leader. Kim went on to ask about development, and Donna had some ideas there, too, but first she asked Kim where *she* thought she needed to grow. While Kim responded, Donna nodded in agreement: Kim wanted to learn more about their company and industry and making sure her support of her colleagues didn't extend to doing their work. Donna also suggested Kim actively seek out more opportunities to get feedback, saying that in her own experience, specific requests helped ensure the focus would be on leadership, not one's personality or looks.

All in all it was a great meeting, and Kim thanked Donna for taking the time.

"I always have time to help others grow," said Donna, "so please get time on my calendar in a few months for another lunch so we can continue this discussion. By then you will have worked with me on the revenue project, so I can ask you for some feedback on my leadership."

Kim couldn't wait.

23
SHEILA CREATES HER OWN PATH

Sheila gave herself a mental pat on the back as she left her favorite restaurant, having just had lunch with her mother. *When I don't take her remarks personally, Mom and I really have a pretty pleasant time together. The key is not reacting, and changing the subject by asking her how she is, and getting her to talk. Even if it's about the food—that's progress!*

In the past few weeks, Sheila had stopped avoiding her mother and had instead tried to reach out to arrange short and manageable outings together. Today she'd surprised her mom by arranging a lunch date.

It's all because I told the coaching group how my mom affects my self-confidence, she mused. *When I mentioned my issues with my mother to the group, Beena and Charles told me how their own parents struggled with letting go and accepting their independence. Beena especially was great. She's had a much harder go of it than me: she had to find a way to respect her Indian culture, where loving and respecting your elders is a given.*

"You are the one who controls how you feel about yourself," Beena had told her. "Not your parents." *Beena has been able to get her father to accept that she has a career and, finally, he has even become proud of her. I know if she can do that, I can, too.*

Hearing about Charles's and Beena's experiences, and realizing that she actually did have a choice, was liberating for Sheila.

As she was driving back to work, she started thinking about the dichotomy between the coach approach, which put all the solving of the problem on the person *with* the problem, and the giving-advice approach of sharing stories like those Charles and Beena had told about similar experiences.

She thought about the two approaches and how different they were, and how useful they both could be.

In thinking back to her first individual coaching session with Jordan—the one where she did all the talking about the relationship with her family—that really set the stage for the ongoing inquiry into how Sheila could change those relationships. Kim had done a great job, too, as her peer coach, making sure she was asking questions and helping Sheila go deeper. By then, Sheila was willing to try some different approaches. Hearing last week how Charles and Beena had struggled with the same thing gave her a sense she wasn't alone, and also that she could change how she was relating to her mom, even if she couldn't change her mom.

Their lunch conversation had been great—Sheila asked her mother all about her job and what her dreams for herself were. She felt as if they were talking as two friends, not parent and child. No one ever really spoke to Sheila's mom about her goals. Sheila was surprised to hear that she was thinking about going back to school.

Now I want to think about taking this into other relationships. Wonder if I can connect that way with my brother, she asked herself.

24
MARIANNE CONFRONTS PATRICK

"How come you're never ready when you need to be?" Marianne berated herself, as her mind raced around looking for the Opening Statement model from *Fierce Conversations*. Patrick had just stopped by her desk and asked her why she had been avoiding him. She knew it was time for a conversation, so she asked if they could meet for a minute in his office. As she followed him back to the office, in a flash she recalled: state the issue, give an example, say how it makes me feel, share what's at stake, identify where I have contributed, and say how much I'd like to resolve the issue, then ask him to respond.[21] *That's close enough*, she thought, as Patrick closed the door and invited her to sit down.

"So, what's up?"

"Well, you know I am in this group coaching program, and I'd like to use a model from one of our books. It requires that I share about sixty seconds' worth of information with you before you get to respond. Is that okay?"

"Shall I time it?"

"If you want," replied Marianne, "as long as you can listen and time."

Here goes nothing, she thought. Taking a deep breath, Marianne began, "I need more room to grow and develop without your ongoing daily involvement in my work." Patrick started to speak, but Marianne raised a warning eyebrow. "For example, yesterday you checked three times on the status of my work on the new performance management model, even though I let you know at the beginning of the day I would have no trouble completing it to your satisfaction by lunchtime. This continual checking and hovering makes me feel like you don't trust me to do a good job and complete my work on time. It causes me to continually second-guess my ability. What's at stake is being able to continue in this job. It feels like I don't have the chance to develop and learn new things and take some risks. Everything has to be perfect and exactly the way you envision it. I admit I have contributed to this by not sharing how I felt sooner and letting things get to the point that I am avoiding you and also not volunteering for anything new. I'd really like for us to be able to work together, because I think this could be a fun job, and I could learn from you if I could be treated more as a valuable contributor rather than someone right out of school."

"Fifty-seven seconds," said Patrick, grinning sheepishly. Then more seriously, he continued, "Wow, I had no idea I was micromanaging you. You do such a great job; it's hard for me not to get involved in what you are working on. I know I do have a perfectionist streak: it drives me crazy, too. And I like to stick my nose everywhere and know what's going on. I guess I've been kind of expecting you to talk to me about it. How are we going to fix this? I really value your contributions and see you as the successor to me in my role here."

Marianne breathed a sigh of relief. She had been afraid that Patrick would take the conversation the wrong way. She wished she had had this conversation months ago, when it first started bugging her. It seemed like he was willing to make things better.

She looked directly at him and said, "I know we can figure this out. Why don't you tell me what you think will help us reach a resolution?"

25
BEENA SHIFTS

What a difference two months makes, Beena thought. Just two months ago, things were really falling apart: her father-in-law's sudden death and her husband leaving suddenly to go to India. She remembered those dark days when she felt she just couldn't do everything anymore.

Part of why she was overwhelmed was work. Learning to let go and let her team step up was a huge reason why she was no longer exhausted. It was really amazing how competent most of her team members were. Why had she thought she was the only one who could lead the team?

Now, Beena was getting home at 5:30 almost every day. She had more time to spend with her boys, who seemed to be growing overnight, and who were almost 4 years old now. Twins! Who would have thought it possible to have a great job and raise twins?

Her thinking was interrupted by her smartphone's buzz. What now? The IM from her project team lead read:

JEFF:
See email today from Arun.

As she opened and read the email, a sense of dread enveloped Beena. They were pushing the deadline up again, and the team had to pull together as soon as possible to figure out how to meet the new date. The meeting was set for first thing tomorrow morning. She had the evening to figure out how to break the news to her team, get them rallied around the new date, and help them sort out options.

Beena decided to do some research on the reasons behind the schedule change. After a few texts with her manager and a detour to Google, she had her answer. Their biggest competitor had just announced the release of a similar enhancement to their software, giving them an advantage in the market. Beena saw she had her answer on how to rally everyone with a vision—they knew their software was better, and with the release that had just moved forward, it would be hard to compete against them.

Besides laying out her vision, Beena also knew she needed to help people sort through their emotions. Everyone was tired, and they had given a lot to the project already. She knew that emotion fueled action, so getting them to talk about how they felt was important. Beena decided to do the one-word check-in,[22] followed by a longer explanation about where everyone was. Once each person had been listened to, it would be the moment to share why the schedule had been changed. She knew it was risky to ask a group of tired and overworked people how they felt—especially in light of the added pressure of a new deadline—but without their emotional commitment, she didn't believe the team would be successful. *Maybe I should start with getting them to describe the best team they have ever been on,* thought Beena. That might help them want to remember what a great team looks and feels like. We really need to work together to push this newest release out the door.

26

RAJ SHARES HIS FEEDBACK

As group members arrived for their group coaching session, Raj was writing on the whiteboard:

- What leadership qualities do you admire?

- How do I stack up?

- When have you seen me at my best?

- What is the one thing you'd like me to keep doing?

- What one thing do you recommend I do differently?

As he finished writing and sat down, the others tried to guess at what Raj was feeling and waited for him to start.

Raj asked everyone to join him in taking a couple of deep breaths. Taking one last breath, he began, "I asked four people to give me feedback—my boss, another peer leader, a person on my team, and an internal client. I was worried at first about taking their time, but all of them seemed really happy to help and kind of touched that I valued them enough to ask."

"I like your questions," Alice said. "They are short, positive, and clear. I hope you are okay with my borrowing some of them."

"Sure," he replied, generously. "Let me continue. So … according to the leaders I spoke with, the top three qualities a leader needs are integrity, confidence, and humility. Those aren't the exact words they used, but those

62

are the themes. And it won't surprise you that the one I scored lowest on was confidence," he said.

"What do you mean by 'scored?'" asked Kim.

"Well, after I finished all my interviews, I emailed my feedback givers a follow-up question, asking them to rate me on a 1 to 10 scale for these three attributes. I did pretty well on integrity—9.75," Raj noted modestly. "Humility I got an 8.5, and confidence … 3. On a positive note, it told me I'd picked the right development goal when I chose leadership presence."

"Wow, buddy, I could add 'courage' to the mix for sure. I think a leader has to have courage, and you've got it, starting us off with your feedback and being so honest," Arthur blurted out.

"Thanks, Arthur. And really thank you to all of you, including Jordan. You make it pretty easy to talk about hard stuff. But let me get to the rest of their feedback, because one thing was pretty surprising. When I asked about when they had seen me at my best, all four of them mentioned something about me being in a good mood: smiling, laughing, or just being happy. I hadn't ever thought about that, but it made sense to me. When I'm relaxed, I smile more, and it's easier for me to share my opinions with confidence."

Everyone nodded, and Jordan commented, "And knowing you, Raj, I have a sense that you did a little reading or research to figure out why."

Raj smiled broadly, "Of course. You know I have really gotten to be a fan of neuroscience since we started this coaching. I've been totally captivated by how our brains, bodies, emotions, and actions are connected. And when I read about smiling, I also found out that *my* brain and emotions are connected to *your* brains." Raj smiled at the puzzled looks of his friends.

"It turns out that when *I* smile, the mirror neurons in *your* brain are activated, and you tend to smile too.[23] I read a lot more than that about smiling, positivity, and productivity on a team. But the bottom line is that when I am happy and smile, I get reinforced by others smiling back. Our emotions are contagious. So it's not too surprising that I'd be more relaxed and more likely to be at my best. I didn't expect it, but the most powerful piece of feedback I got about what to keep doing and what to do differently was to smile more. And I am happy to do that!"

"Thanks for showing us the way to take in feedback, Raj. You are an inspiration," Kim said, summing up what everyone was thinking.

27
ALICE CAN'T WAIT

Alice couldn't wait to talk to Jordan. Their midpoint one-on-one coaching session had shifted a few times due to Alice's schedule, and they were finally going to be able to talk that afternoon.

"So, what's up?" asked Jordan.

"A bunch!" exclaimed Alice. "I'm still chewing over what I shared in the last group session about the project team meeting. It makes such a difference to listen. It still surprises me."

Jordan asked, "How can you reinforce what you are learning?"

"Well, the main thing is to keep setting my intention to listen and then notice what happens. I've gotten really curious to see what happens when I lean back. Almost always, something interesting comes up."

"Anything else?"

"Yes. I'm getting some great support from others when I tell them my intentions before a meeting. It helps my team members understand why I am behaving differently and gives them a chance to do something else too. I even got a compliment from my challenging team member, Bill, after our last meeting. He said that based on my example, he wanted to sign up for the next leadership coaching program after the pilot."

"Hey, that's great," Jordan said. "I love it that you are so open about your own development. Is Bill one of the leaders you will ask to give you feedback?"

"Hey, that's a thought. I hadn't considered him because Bill and I butt heads so often, but now that we are talking about our leadership development, maybe that would be a good idea. He's got to pass your test of being someone I admire as a leader. Though I guess that because we are just alike—another recent insight of mine—I *have* to say I admire him!"

During the silence that followed, both Jordan and Alice enjoyed reflecting on how Alice was growing. And both silently wondered what would happen next.

28

ARTHUR TALKS TO TIFFANY

"Tiffany, I really appreciate you meeting with me. As I mentioned in my email, I'm trying to get feedback so I can be a better leader. I'm asking people whose leadership I admire for their input."

"I'm not really a leader, Arthur. Why would you want to talk to me instead of someone in a leadership role here?" asked Tiffany.

"I realize you aren't a leader in your official position, Tiffany, but our conversation a couple of weeks ago was really valuable to me. And I need to do this feedback formally for the group coaching program I am in. We are learning that leadership isn't a role or a position. Instead it's really a way of being with others that makes them want to follow you."

"Yes, I'm willing, then," she chimed in. "I've seen in the past few weeks that you're trying to operate differently. And that's what matters to me. It's been better coming to work; I didn't even follow through with that other job application I was considering."

Arthur acknowledged Tiffany, "Thank you for your trust. I'm eager to learn and get better. So here's my first question: what does it take to move from being a manager to being a leader?"

"Actually, you're beginning to do it," said Tiffany. "I think true leadership is about asking instead of telling your people what to do. It's motivating us to find our own answers instead of giving us yours. You've done a lot better with that on this project we're working on now, even in our meetings. If we had recorded a meeting a month or two ago, it would have shown you talking and giving directions almost 100 percent of the time. Now you ask us what we think, and you make sure we all have a chance to put our two cents in. You are probably only talking about a third of the time. You are still making the decisions, which is fine, but now we can all buy in to the decisions because we have had a chance to be heard.

"I also think the change from manager to leader requires that you have a vision for what you want and that you share that dream. That is what motivates me: following someone who has a vision for where we are going. I don't feel like I know anything about what you aspire to, at least not yet."

Arthur swallowed hard, and simply said, "Fair enough. Thank you. This next question is easier; well, for me anyway. What is something you think I do well, and that you want me to keep doing?"

"Lately it seems like you are sharing more about what you are thinking—even if you don't know the answer. I want you to keep doing that, because it makes a difference. I can follow your logic. I also like it when you admit you don't know something. Not everyone likes that, because sometimes we want you to tell us what to do. Still, it's reassuring to feel that when you do tell us what to do, you aren't faking it anymore, and that is a good thing. It's also easier for us to speak up when you don't know, because we feel that all ideas will be valued, and that one of us might offer the best solution. I want you to keep doing that. I've learned something from you there."

Arthur noticed he was starting to enjoy the conversation because they were having a conversation, a dialogue. In the process, he was realizing that his team members could indeed think for themselves. In fact, they *had* been thinking for themselves. He had been so busy trying to be the boss with all the answers that he hadn't noticed how smart and how thoughtful Tiffany was.

While he knew it would take him a while to shift his behavior, Arthur felt like he was making progress, and that he knew the road map going forward. He was thankful for Tiffany's good ideas—it was going to be easier relying on his team more and not having to have all the answers himself. And he was going to need to spend more time thinking about where they were going, and how to provide some context for their work and where it fit into the bigger picture.

29
CHARLES WONDERS—
WAS IT TOO EASY?

Charles was distraught. He raked his hands through his hair and muttered to himself.

"What was that?" asked his project co-lead Keenan as he came into Charles's office. "Were you talking to yourself?"

"I was just saying that it seemed too easy."

"What?"

"Oh, nothing."

Keenan persisted. "Well, it's obviously something, Charles. You are looking crazy. What's up?"

Charles put his hands up in surrender and said, "I don't even know anymore. Things had been getting better and better, and even Ed was happy. Now I just don't know anymore. Maybe it was just too easy. Maybe nothing really changed at all."

"Well, something must have happened. Tell me."

Charles tried to think back about what started first. His customer Ed calling up first thing and raging about an outage set things off, and then half his staff members were absent because of a project management training session. Why was the training scheduled this week, of all times, when they had a major release due? He must have been muttering out loud again, because Keenan was looking worriedly his way.

"Hey, man, how can I help?"

And what help did he need? Charles knew he needed to short-circuit the stress and overwhelm or he would never be able to lead the team and get things back on track. He took a deep breath and said, "Let me just take a walk around the building—ten minutes—and then when I get back we can talk."

"Sure thing."

Charles coached himself as he rounded the first outside corner of the building. He practiced breathing and cycling through his five senses one at a time, seeing everything in color and clearly, hearing the birdsong and traffic noise and the sound of his feet, savoring the smell of the freshly cut grass and hot pavement, tasting the metallic tang of stress in his mouth, and feeling the heat of the pavement through his loafers and the brush of his arms against his side. There, that was better; he felt much calmer and more alive. He deliberately slowed his breathing—three seconds on the in breath, five on the out breath. Now he was really calm.

So could he make a choice to experience this and not get totally over-stressed? He was now curious to find out.

When he returned to his office, he could immediately see something had changed. Keenan greeted him with "Ed just called, and you will never guess what happened. He actually apologized, not realizing that it wasn't you on the phone. I told him I would pass it along and that you would call him back. Can you believe it?"

Charles could and couldn't believe it.

30

KIM SHARES HER FEEDBACK

Kim had decided to follow Raj's lead and share her feedback with the others. As everyone walked in to the next group coaching session, she handed each person a sheet of paper titled "What I Learned." As they sat down together, Charles scanned down the page and saw her list of questions:

What are the most important aspects of being a leader?

What do you see as my best leadership traits?

Where am I falling short in my leadership?

What's the one most important thing for me to be focusing on?

How will I know when I've been successful?

Below each question, Kim had included the responses she'd received from the three people she'd interviewed.

"Welcome, everyone. Before we start in with Kim's feedback," Jordan commented, "who has a check-in question that will help us all to get present and focused?"

Arthur offered, "How about: how hard was it to ask for feedback and who chickened out?"

Everyone laughed.

"Can I amend that?" Beena asked. "What about: what two or three emotions do I have about my feedback?"

Most of the group members nodded their heads in agreement.

Alice began with "Anxiety. Determination. Anger, at myself mostly."

"For me, it's excitement, curiosity, and patience," Beena said.

"Curiosity for me too," Charles chimed in. "And regret. I've made a lot of mistakes."

Arthur said, "Nervous—because asking for feedback when you know you aren't doing well is hard. And proud that I was able to."

They continued around the circle, each sharing a bit of their experience in asking for and listening to feedback. When it came back to Kim, she noted, "Wow, I'm really amazed how different this exercise has been for each of us. My three words are hopeful, relieved, surprised."

She continued, pointing to her printed notes, "You all can see the feedback I got. I tried to capture their comments verbatim. There are a couple of themes that stood out. One is that everyone thinks I'm nice, but they don't really see 'niceness' as a powerful leadership attribute. Ouch. Two people think I say 'yes' too much, that it confuses people around me because they don't really know what I am most interested in or skilled at. They aren't sure when they are piling on too much. Setting priorities came up in all three of my conversations, and that really does make me hopeful. I've been acting like I have to do everything, and each person I talked to told me I just have to communicate what I'm working on and what others can expect from me. When I think I can't, or shouldn't, work on something, I should say that. I know that ought to have been obvious to me, but it wasn't. So it was a big relief, and it makes my next steps more clear. What do you all think I'm missing?"

Marianne had starred a couple of things on the page while Kim had been talking, and now made eye contact with her. "Well, it seems like you kind of missed the boat on a couple of pretty big things here." When she saw Kim's look of concern, Marianne went on, "You didn't mention that you also got comments that you are an inspiration to others, and that your hard work and positive attitude help to motivate everyone around you. And that you are empathetic and help others out when they need it. That might be important not to overlook."

"Great observations, everyone," Jordan put in. "What did you come up with, Kim, as far as your action plan?"

"I have two priorities," Kim responded. "Results focus. And teamwork. For results focus, what I am going to do is to plan each Monday what outcomes I want by the end of the week. That will keep me on track and give me a way to evaluate my success each week. For teamwork, I know this will sound strange, but my plan is to say no at least three times a week. Because I say yes to everything and everyone, I've ended up not being clear about what I am really good at and passionate about. By saying no sometimes, I feel like I'll be more effective on the teams I'm on, and others will have the chance to step up and say yes to the things they really want to do."

"Well, you're definitely helping me not to be so nervous about this," Arthur commented. "Thanks to you and Raj for going first with your feedback. It's embarrassing to say it, but I have been avoiding talking about how I am doing as a leader, particularly since I already know what people are going to say. After talking to Tiffany, I was proud that I finished one of my interviews, but couldn't make myself do the others. Thanks for showing the way for me to get back to it."

A few minutes later, group members headed out in twos and threes, continuing their conversations. Sheila stayed behind with Jordan, scheduling her next one-on-one coaching session. "I have a lot I want to talk about, so let's make it soon."

31

SHEILA FIGURES SOME THINGS OUT

"Thanks for being available so quickly," Sheila told Jordan as they entered the small conference room. "I feel like I'm on the verge of something in my leadership, and I want some help sorting through it."

Jordan smiled. "Go on."

"I don't know if you remember when we started coaching how self-critical I was, and how hard it was for me to turn off that internal voice that said whatever I did was not enough."

Jordan nodded.

"Well, I've gotten much more confident over these last few months. And it's helped in a lot of my relationships, both at work and with my family." Sheila looked to make sure that Jordan was following her. "The thing is, I am still not very good at holding others accountable. I'm hard on myself, and inside I'm critical of others, too. But I don't really hold them accountable. I let them off the hook, even though inside I am judging them and deciding not to ever work with them again after they don't come through for me. I want to work on that, and I need some coaching to decide how."

"What have you tried so far?" Jordan prompted her.

"The thing that has helped me most is seeing what I am actually doing right, and what others are doing right, too. Instead of focusing on inadequacies, I've been focusing on what is already good and how to build on that. I just jot down in my schedule a couple of 'wins' in each meeting or working session. I focus on what I want instead of what I don't want. That has helped a lot."[24]

As Jordan listened, Sheila went on, "I'm focusing on the positive with my brother and my mom, too. It drives me crazy that my brother isn't independent at age 30, and it probably drives him crazy, too. Now instead of being sarcastic or just ignoring him, I thank him when he does something nice, like getting us a snack when I'm visiting. And I ask a lot of questions and really listen when he mentions going out. I actually think it's making a difference. He seems more relaxed around me, and he isn't as guarded. He even asked me to help him post his résumé on one of the job websites. And he went to his college career center and took a vocational interest survey so he could figure out what he wants to do. Instead of my usual sarcastic, 'It's about time,' I was excited for him. And I think he felt it."

"You sound like you are really pleased about how your relationship with your brother is changing," Jordan commented.

"I am! And I'm using a similar approach with my direct reports, really focusing on noticing the things they are doing that I appreciate, and letting them know I'm noticing. And then praising them when they have an idea or initiate something. I feel good about that."

"Sounds like a lot of things are going well for you, Sheila. So what's not quite right yet?"

"I still don't know how to hold my team accountable when they don't do what they agree to, or don't meet a deadline or complete a client deliverable. I feel like I'm not being a good leader if I don't hold them accountable."

"Yes, I saw you added that to your coaching action plan. So what do you want to do?"

"That's what I wanted to talk to you about. I've started to do it already. I ask them what is going right and where they succeeded. And when they don't meet expectations, I just ask what got in the way and what they will do next. Instead of criticizing, I hold them accountable by asking what they want to accomplish and what they will do. It feels a lot better to me, and some of them are coming up with some pretty good answers and actually following through. Could it be that simple?"

"Are you getting the results you want?" Jordan asked.

"I am," she responded.

"What does that tell you?" Jordan persisted.

"I think it tells me I might have figured out accountability, and it's not nearly as hard as I thought."

32
MARIANNE AND BEENA COACH EACH OTHER

Marianne and Beena were having their last scheduled peer coaching session. Marianne had just finished telling Beena how glad she was that she finally talked to Patrick about his overinvolvement in her work. To think that she was recently thinking about leaving her job, and that now it looked like she could grow right along with it.

Beena was impressed. She didn't know Patrick well, but she had heard a lot from Marianne about how he was stifling her. She was really glad for her friend that he had taken the conversation well. Goodness knows, Marianne had rehearsed enough!

Marianne finished up by saying, "You know all those rehearsals? Well, I think that the more we talked about this, the clearer I was that I had to have the conversation no matter what. Just like Susan Scott says, 'The conversation is the relationship,'[25] and ours was really suffering. Thanks for listening to me. I don't think I would have had the courage to step into this without your help."

"No worries," said Beena. "I learned a lot, too. It seems like there are lots of opportunities everywhere to have a 'fierce conversation.'"

"Sounds like a loaded comment," countered Marianne. "I think you might have something to share."

"How did you guess?" exploded Beena. "I really need some help with Arun. You know him, my boss's boss, the head guy around here for technology. He seems to think everything can be accomplished overnight, and he doesn't understand how exhausted the team is. We can't keep going on like this, and I've run out of ideas. I asked the team to pull together for this last push, and they did a great job, but guess what? He has changed the project specs again, and now it's back to the drawing board."

"But I thought the big push was to get the release out to get the jump on the competition?"

"So did we, but now he wants to make sure that what we are coding is frontwards compatible to this big new idea he has to move everything to the cloud." Beena saw Marianne's look of puzzlement, so she brushed away further explanations and said, "Don't worry about what that means technically. The point is that we have to rework most of what we have already done."

"I can see how frustrating that is." Marianne thought of her own frustration when Ellen, Patrick's boss, changed some critical metrics on a key project. But she didn't voice her experience. Instead she asked, "What are you thinking of doing?"

"What I really need to do is share with Arun how upset the team is … but maybe he knows that. I wish he wasn't so arrogant about everything. If he could just show some empathy toward the team."

"Have you asked him for that?"

"That's what I would really call a 'fierce conversation,'" Beena replied.

"Why?" Now Marianne was getting curious. She couldn't see how that was a problem, but she didn't know Arun and she wasn't Beena. It was hard not to give advice here and tell Beena what she would do, but learning about coaching from Jordan had convinced Marianne that giving advice wouldn't work.

"It seems like Arun really doesn't care about the people, just his own ideas," explained Beena.

They sat in silence for a moment.

"Of course, he can be rather compelling when he gets going about the cloud."

Another silence. It was hard for Marianne not to jump in with a solution, but she knew that Beena had to figure something out for herself. Marianne also knew that as much as she wanted to help solve the problem, the best help she could give was asking questions and being there with Beena.

"Here's what would be a fierce conversation," Beena finally said with a small grin. "Getting Arun to come talk to the team about the cloud—just the cloud, nothing about how it was his idea, or that we have to meet the deadline, or that we will fail if we don't. Only the cloud!"

"Would some rehearsal help?" Marianne asked.

"Oh, yes!" said Beena, happily.

33
RAJ HAS HIS DOUBTS

Raj sat at his desk, reading an email from Sheila and feeling reluctant to get up and head out to his final peer coaching session with Alice. *I'm really going to miss these conversations,* he thought. *I'm not sure I've really mastered what I was hoping to at the beginning of all this.*

His smartphone alerted him to an IM:

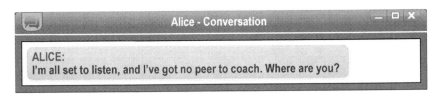

Alice - Conversation

ALICE:
I'm all set to listen, and I've got no peer to coach. Where are you?

With a sigh, Raj got up and headed out of the building to meet Alice.

Today, they had decided to go on a long walk together as they talked. Both of them thought they wanted to get more exercise, and Raj was really aware of how much walking helped him think, breathe, and talk. Alice greeted him, and they set off for a walk around the small lake behind their corporate offices.

They walked in silence for the first quarter mile before Raj said what he'd been thinking: "I'm not done yet, Alice. I'm not where I want to be. I'm happy with how much I've learned and with some small successes in my meeting presentations, but I've got a long way to go. I think we're stopping too soon."

Alice listened, waiting for Raj to say more.

"I mean, you and the others are really on a roll. You've got your team trusting you more since you've learned to lean back and listen. Charles has had a complete attitude adjustment and seems like he's handling the load much better. He even asked his girlfriend to marry him now that he doesn't feel so overwhelmed at work. And did you get Sheila's email about accountability with her business partners? That blew me away."

Alice nodded, and Raj continued, "But me, I've just taken a few baby steps. Reading books and understanding neuroscience doesn't cut it when I'm in a big meeting. I still get nervous when a lot is on the line with a presentation. It's hard for me to get in the habit of breathing and calming myself so I can talk more slowly and clearly. I'm afraid I'll slide back into my old habits."

Alice nodded. "To tell you the truth, Raj, I'm scared, too. When we started, I thought five months seemed like a long time to be doing this. Now it seems way too short. Just now, I almost interrupted you while you were talking. I've got a long way to go on listening, too."

"Jordan said we could keep meeting even after the coaching group ended. Do you think anyone would be up for that?" Raj asked.

"I'm not sure," Alice replied. "We've all got a lot going on. Maybe people will feel like they are too busy to continue."

Raj stopped and looked at Alice, "Are *you* too busy?"

"You know, that's a great question, Raj. I don't think I am. I think this is probably just as important as anything else I'm supposed to be doing. Let's see if we can figure something out. It doesn't seem like either of us is done yet."

34

ALICE GETS FORCE-FED FEEDBACK

I was really excited about this coaching program, Alice thought, *and now I almost hate it. I can't believe I opened myself up to this level of scrutiny. And I can't believe I even told Raj I wanted to continue the peer coaching. I'm done with this.*

Almost everyone Alice had talked to about her leadership brand had given her the same sort of feedback: "Alice, you have good ideas but you are too pushy, too forceful, too aggressive." The one that really set her off was this one: "Alice, you make people want to push back because you are pushing forward so hard."

The one person she had left to interview was Bill, who was bound to give her a load of it. They had been adversaries forever, always competing for the same roles and always trying to beat out the other's ideas. Why had she chosen to talk to Bill? Oh, yeah, it was the coach's fault. It was Jordan's idea! One more reason to hate the coaching program.

Well, here goes nothing, she thought. *He is going to show up in my office right about now...* And there he was.

Bill had a big grin on his face. "Whaddup?" he asked, as he sauntered into the room. "You look cross."

"I *am* cross. This coaching program has brought out the worst in me and everyone else. I asked for feedback, and everyone keeps blasting me over the same thing. I bet you will, too."

"Well, actually, I was going to compliment you. See, I realize that you and I are a lot alike. We have big ideas and big energy, and we want others to see what we see. But when you started sitting back and letting others step forward, I could see how your creating space worked to help connect with others and get them in the game. It was pretty amazing to see how energized our project team got."

Alice looked at Bill with surprise. "Go on."

"Well, that's about it. I was going to compliment you on self-management and courage, and for the results you're getting out of the team. I'd actually like you to help me learn to hold off a bit myself and coach me so the rest of the team can step up. Would you do that?"

"Of course," Alice replied. "And there is this great group coaching program you can get into if TE offers it again. I would recommend it."

35

IS COACHING FINISHED?

"I can't believe we are already at the end of the coaching for our group here," Patrick began his meeting with Jordan. "It seems like such a short time, and so much has changed. Not easy for sure, especially not the transformations that Marianne had in mind for me!"

Jordan smiled. "You did an amazing job modeling what a great boss does when he gets painful feedback."

"Well, it definitely provided motivation for me to shift how I manage Marianne *and* others. I had no idea that she felt I was micromanaging her until she had the courage to begin that dialogue with me. I started realizing that I was in too deep with several people, and that was preventing me from getting my real work done. I am never going to get promoted to an executive role if I keep on inserting myself in everyone else's details and decisions.

"I'm also hearing from others how well the leaders are developing. Raj is speaking up much more and has volunteered to give several presentations. Arthur's team has calmed down about his leadership—at least they aren't coming to me to complain. Bill wants to be in the next group coaching cohort, and he and Alice seem to be new best friends. Donna is asking for Kim to help her in a key project for the company—I could go on and on, but these are just a few of the stories I have heard. What a success this group coaching pilot has been, Jordan. You really made me look good."

"I'm grateful you are passing along what you are hearing, Patrick. I love coaching leaders in a group, because they can help each other and give each other feedback. The other thing that happens is that long after the program is over, they will be supporting each other's leadership development."

Jordan continued, "Feedback helps me keep improving the program, too. Can I specifically ask you what are the top three impacts you saw for the program?"

Patrick launched in without hesitation, "Number one is something you really didn't promise, but it's had a huge impact. It's the confidence these leaders have now. Some of them weren't fully trusted before because they lacked confidence in themselves. Now it feels like each one of them is willing to take risks, confront others, and is even confident enough to say when they don't know something. I'm sure all the tools help—like how to have a difficult conversation—but a big piece is that they just know themselves better. That helps them to consciously bring the best of themselves to Tech Environments every day."

Patrick continued, "The second thing is also something you didn't explicitly tell me to expect. It has to do with openness. I know a big part of the coaching program was them asking for feedback. They all did that, and they listened to the feedback they received. But I mean more than that when I say openness. Charles and Arthur and Sheila, all of them, really, are more willing to learn from others and to ask for help. They share when they've made a mistake, and it makes it safe for others to acknowledge issues, too. Their increased openness has had a huge effect. It lets them keep growing.

"Number three has to be collaboration. As you know, the leaders in this coaching effort come from three different levels in our organization. Some of them have a lot of authority, and others are pretty new as supervisors. Everyone has to be able to lead a team, and to follow someone else's lead when they aren't the expert. Having peer coaches helped them see that they can accomplish a lot more and get past their blind spots when they collaborate. That was huge for me to see happening. Is that the kind of thing you are looking for when you ask about impacts?"

"That's great," Jordan responded. "The results are a little different for each group and every organization. But what you are telling me rings true.

Let me also ask you a challenging question: what *didn't* go the way you had hoped? What would you recommend I do differently next time?"

Patrick didn't respond immediately. "Well, I was going to say it was a lot of work and time, maybe too much. I think you assigned two books for them to read, and then there was the TAIS assessment at the beginning, and peer coaching, and the group sessions, and asking for feedback, and sharing their leadership action plan with a manager. It felt like a lot to ask of people who are already busy. When I say it out loud, though, I am realizing that maybe the reason for the great results is that the program was pretty intense. I know one or two of them didn't get all the reading done, yet all of them talked about the group coaching and wished there were more sessions. And Beena in particular mentioned her one-on-one sessions with you and her peer coaching with Marianne. So they all seemed to manage the time commitment okay. I've already heard from a couple of them that they are going to continue their peer coaching, and they want to find a way to keep gathering as a group, too. So maybe I'm the only one who thought it was too much work. It might not be as effective if you trimmed too much."

"Thank you, Patrick. It's helpful to hear what you noticed. Let me know if you think of anything else. I am always open to improving the model and the tools. Feedback makes us all better.

"Okay, last question," Jordan announced. "What, if anything, do you plan to do to support these eight leaders as they continue to work their leadership action plans and apply what they've learned?"

Patrick smiled at this question. "I've already thought about that. I want them to be teaching others some of the tools they have been using. Lazy Coaching, in particular. I think that can help any leader avoid getting into a telling mode. It might even help our sales team. It seems like that approach makes for a much more collaborative atmosphere. I was going to ask Marianne if she would invite a couple of the group members

86

to do a manager training workshop to teach and demonstrate the Lazy Coaching model."

"I know Marianne would like that, Patrick, especially if you let *her* take the lead on it," Jordan said. She and Patrick both smiled, remembering Marianne's request that Patrick empower and trust her more. "And Raj would love practicing his presentation skills."

Patrick continued, "Two more things I've been thinking about for us to build on this experience. First, I want to start another group a couple of months from now. I plan to see who's interested and do interviews this time. I know that Bill, on Alice's team, wants to be a part of it. And I've been approached by a couple of others who knew about the program because they were asked for feedback by the group members. I think coaching is pretty appealing to a lot of people, especially now that they see how others have benefited. So let's plan on another group starting in the early spring. Maybe that could offer a mentoring opportunity, too, for the group who just went through this one."

Jordan nodded enthusiastically. "I'd love to coach another group here at Tech Environments. You've been a great partner. Nothing would please me more than seeing you and Ellen realize your vision for a culture that keeps everyone growing and developing as leaders."

"Thank you, Jordan. Thanks to you I've gotten great feedback from my boss Ellen for launching this group coaching pilot. I'm looking forward to working on the next one with you."

Patrick and Jordan shook hands and Jordan headed out of his office, both looking forward to their next meeting.

PART 2

THE LEADERSHIP TEAM TAKES THE PLUNGE

36

IS TEAM COACHING THE ANSWER?

Ellen had a problem in the C-suite. The last few years had been great, with profits up, associate engagement scores up, and a well-functioning senior leadership team that she was delighted to be a part of as the newly promoted Chief People Officer.

But she had blinked, and now everything was going wrong. Ellen had taken her eye off the team because she had been heavily involved in recruiting a new Chief Marketing Officer, Donna. It had taken forever to find someone with Donna's experience, and now that she was finally on the job, Ellen was helping her get up to speed.

Then there was the matter of Edgar's promotion to Chief Risk Officer, which hadn't been very smooth. Who could really blame Edgar when the jump from manager to executive was so high at Tech Environments? And he wasn't getting any attention from their CEO, Jack. Jack had been totally distracted lately by the economic downturn and a hungry new competitor in their market who was trying to buy market share. To make matters worse on the leadership team, the CTO, Arun, was advocating a substantial shift in their strategy, and he was butting heads with longtime CFO Ted. Arun wanted more investment in technology, and Ted was having none of that. Now Ted was threatening to move up his retirement date again, which would be a disaster.

It seemed to Ellen that Jack was also suffering from an atypical crisis of confidence about the overall direction of the firm. Strategic vision had always been the CEO's strong suit, and he'd always been able to rely on a focused executive team to embrace his vision and execute it. Now that the leadership team was squabbling and either getting up to speed or struggling with their day-to-day operations, they didn't seem to align on anything.

Ellen sighed as the next appointment on her calendar pinged. In fifteen minutes she had to meet with Patrick and Jordan about furthering the leadership development agenda at Tech Environments. Ellen wondered if it was too late to postpone the meeting—she truly didn't have time—but ruefully admitted that it was probably too late to cancel unless there was an emergency. An IM from Jack flashed across Ellen's computer screen, and she wondered if the emergency she longed for was now happening.

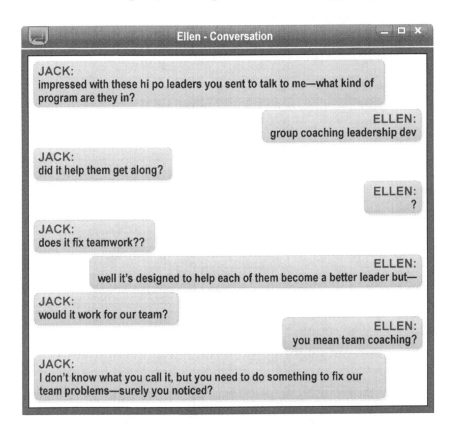

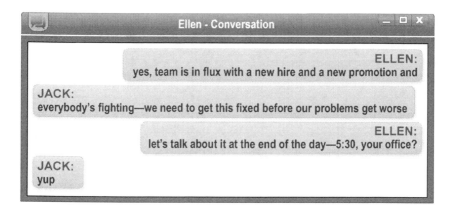

Out of the corner of her eye, Ellen saw Patrick and Jordan arrive at her outer office.

GETTING STARTED

E llen was in a rush to get an email out before the first team coaching session, which was scheduled in fifteen minutes. But the flashing blue IM box caught her eye, and she quickly scanned what Jack had typed.

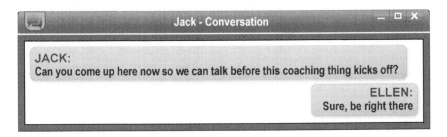

JACK:
Can you come up here now so we can talk before this coaching thing kicks off?

ELLEN:
Sure, be right there

Ellen knew he was nervous, because even contemplating something like this was way outside Jack's comfort zone, even though he had agreed to the team coaching. But since Jordan had met with each person on the leadership team in a one-on-one coaching session, most of them were now on board with their plan, Ellen thought. Or rather, she hoped. She wondered how Jack's one-on-one coaching had gone. Funny that he didn't talk to her about it.

Jack was pacing around his office when she arrived. "I am just not sure about this, Ellen. What exactly are we going to be doing? Will this be embarrassing? I don't want to talk about feelings—not sure I want to share mine, since I am not very happy right now." Ellen hoped she hadn't winced upon hearing that last remark. Sometimes Jack was pretty clueless.

"I don't think we have to worry about anything. You said yourself that the team had to start getting along and working together, and this is our opportunity to get some help to accomplish that," she observed. "Besides, the pilot group coaching program went extremely well."

"I don't know why you couldn't have taken care of that for the leadership team."

Since Jack wasn't really asking a question, Ellen didn't answer. She *did* feel responsible for how the team functioned, but that was more than she could actually deliver. Which led Ellen to think about her conversation with Jordan and the leadership development goals she had set for herself: to be more strategic and to stop trying to manage what she could not control. Working in a technology company these past few years had really pushed her into daily firefighting and a reactive, short-term focus. And of course Jack looked to her to solve any and every people problem. He was quick to ask her, "Why did I make you Chief People Officer, Ellen?" And then he would answer his own question: "You are in charge of people, just like the CTO is in charge of technology." She knew it wasn't that simple, yet she hadn't really been able to push back on that question successfully. Ellen did know that as long as Jack and everyone else on the team held her responsible for their functioning, they wouldn't be accountable themselves.

Jack interrupted her thoughts by brushing past her as he circled the room. She noticed that there were light wear marks forming in the carpet along his path. She smiled, and forced herself to listen to his next question: "So what will happen today, Ellen?" Before she could answer, Edgar, Arun, Ted, Donna, and Jordan, talking and laughing, came into the adjacent conference room.

Shrugging at Ellen as if to say, "Never mind," Jack detoured over to the conference room and invited everyone to sit at the table. They all found their places, with Jordan sitting opposite Jack.

Jordan began: "Jack, would you like to say a few words to get us started?" Without hesitation, he launched into his reasons for bringing in team coaching and what he hoped to accomplish. Ellen was impressed with Jack's willingness to share his disappointment in their lack of teamwork and leadership. She had forgotten how inspiring Jack could be when he decided to be vulnerable. Jack continued by telling the team that he didn't have the answers, and maybe not even the questions, but he was willing to be accountable and learn how to be a better leader, too. Everyone paid close attention to his remarks, then looked at Jordan expectantly.

"By now," Jordan said, "you have all met with me individually, talked about your strengths as leaders, and come up with a development goal for yourself. We will be sharing those at our next team coaching session, but today what I'd like to do is to pair you up with a peer coach. You'll spend much of the time we have scheduled for team coaching today with your peer coach, discussing with each other what you shared with me: your leadership development goal and your strengths based on feedback you have gotten in the past and what you learned from the assessment. If you have time, I also want you and your peer coach to talk about what you think the strengths of the team are and how the team as a whole needs to change to be more successful. When we meet next week, we will all share what you have discussed with your peer coach. Please keep notes if you need to and be ready to share with the larger group. Any questions?"

Silence filled the room as they looked uneasily at each other. Jack finally broke it by saying, "Okay, so we are going to be in pairs today. Ellen and I are together. Who else?"

"Actually, Jack," Jordan spoke confidently, "I have you and Edgar together for peer coaching. And then Arun and Ted, and Ellen and Donna. Since you all have already scheduled the time to be here today, I'd like you to stay here in the executive suite for your first peer coaching meetings. There's plenty of space to have some privacy—and that way you won't get interrupted."

Jordan went on, "Between each team coaching session, you should plan for about two hours' worth of homework, and one of those hours will be spent with your peer coach focusing on your leadership development goals and doing other assignments together. So let's get started with that today. Any questions?"

"Only one," muttered Ted to himself. "Why did you assign Arun to me?"

38
EDGAR AND JACK ROLL

Edgar sat down, gazing at the screen of his smartphone. Jack waited, expecting Edgar to look up when he'd finished. Instead, Edgar continued to scroll through his text messages.

After a couple of seconds, Jack spoke up. "Got something blowing up in Risk Management today, Edgar?"

Edgar looked up at his boss, disconcerted. "Uh, no. Actually, I was getting caught up on all the work I left hanging by coming to this meeting—now it looks like we aren't even having the team meeting."

Jack was immediately irritated, and he was not sure how to read Edgar. Taking a breath to gather himself, he spoke calmly, but with some energy in his voice. "How about we get started with our peer coaching, Edgar, like Jordan just asked us to do. After all, I wasn't excluding myself when I said I was disappointed in how we are functioning as a leadership team. I am trusting that what she is asking us to do will help each of us and all of us together."

Chastened, Edgar set down his phone. "Okay, Jack. What do you have in mind?"

"Why don't you start by telling me your leadership strengths, the ones you shared with Jordan, and your own goal for this team coaching?" Jack asked.

Edgar picked up his phone again, then glanced at Jack and reassured him, "I'm just pulling up the notes I made for myself. Here we go. For my goal, I've got 'Figure out how to get everyone in the risk department on the same page.' I'm thinking about some processes and procedures that will ensure no one goes off the page. Then for my strengths I put down 'risk reduction business and legal expertise; directness; consistency.'" He looked up again. "How about you?"

Jack smiled. "Not so fast, Edgar. I want to understand what you're saying. You said your leadership goal is to get everyone in Risk Management on the same page. I get why that's important to you. But what's your goal for *yourself* as a leader? You're new to this role, and I have to believe you've got some things you want to develop in yourself as a leader. That goal sounds like it's more about them than you."

"Yeah, Jordan asked me pretty much the same thing. But to be honest with you, Jack, I'm right where I want to be. You just promoted me, and that's the goal I've been working toward: Chief Risk Officer. So now I want to do the job, and I want to do it well. It seems like first things first: get everyone on the same page so we anticipate and manage Tech Environments' risks."

"Okay, then, let me ask you a different question. What does your team think about this? Are they all on board with the risk strategy you have outlined?"

"Uh, no, not yet," Edgar said, clearing his throat. "There might be a couple who we end up letting go if they can't get on board. But I haven't made any decisions about that yet."

Jack answered quickly, "Well, I am pretty new to peer coaching and team coaching, Edgar, but I have the sense that it starts with us as individual leaders and maybe being willing to tell each other the truth. I wonder if you gave it more thought you could come up with something you could develop to be more effective as a leader in this new role."

Edgar shrugged and looked helplessly at Jack. "Honestly, Jack, I just want to do a good job. I want to protect the company from risk. That's what you trust me to do."

"Well, that's an honest answer, Edgar, and I'm also going to trust you to do some thinking and come up with a way you personally want to grow.

But I can hear you don't have that right now. Are you willing to work on figuring out a leadership development goal before we meet again?"

Edgar nodded, and Jack went on, "Okay, well, for me, part of how I am seeing this peer coaching is that we do get to be honest with each other here, maybe even take a few risks that we might not be as comfortable taking with the whole group. And I want you to know that I need your feedback and your help. I believe I've been less than a good leader for our team and our company the past couple of months. I know I've been a good leader in the past, but right now we need something different, and I'm not sure what."

Edgar interrupted, trying to help Jack. "So your goal is to identify the best leadership practice to use?"

Jack spoke slowly, "No, and yes. My goal isn't like something you'd read in a management book—find and implement the best leadership practices for the stage of your business. My leadership goal is actually to be vulnerable, ask for help, and recognize I don't have all the answers. That's what I've shared with Jordan so far. As a leader, I want to be a good partner to each of you and to ask each of you to be a good partner to me and each other. I want it to be safe for me on this leadership team not to have all the answers. At least not right now. I don't want to jump quickly to a solution. I think it's important to really understand where you're each coming from—what your strengths are and where you want to get better—along with what Tech Environments is good at and how we can make it better. Only if we all contribute our best can we move this company forward and make the tough decisions. What do you think, Edgar? Are you up to helping me with that goal?"

"I'm not really sure, Jack. It sounds like you are saying you want to be free to be kind of clueless. No offense, but that sounds risky to me for the head of a company. As your Chief Risk Officer, you pay me to know everything about the risks and to fill in the gaps quickly when I don't know. What you are saying doesn't make a lot of sense to me. To commit to a goal of being vulnerable, not knowing, of just trying to understand, instead of doing something about it? It doesn't sound very leader-like to me. Again, I'm just being honest with you, Jack. As I said earlier, one of my strengths is my directness."

"Fair enough, Edgar. I guess that's a start."

Just then, Edgar's phone alarm chimed, and they both knew they were about out of time and should rejoin the group. As he stood up, Jack said, "By the way, the three strengths that came up for me were committed, decisive, and competitive."

Edgar responded with a nod as he got up. "Yes, I can see all of those. Even before I was part of this team, I saw those things about you. Thanks for sharing that, Jack. I'll be curious to see how this process goes. I wish Jordan would give us some more direction."

ELLEN AND DONNA COMPARE NOTES

In the far corner of the conference room, Ellen and Donna smiled widely at each other as they moved two chairs facing each other, both happy and surprised that they had been paired up for peer coaching. "If this were the old days," remarked Donna, "Jordan never would have paired us up—not politically correct to put the only two women together."

"And if it were the *really* old days, we wouldn't even be here," joked Ellen. They shared a rueful laugh.

Ellen spoke again, "I really enjoyed meeting you in the interview process, Donna, but I feel like we have hardly spoken since."

"I know," Donna replied. "I can't believe I've been here for three months. In some ways it seems like three years, in others, three minutes."

"Can you tell me more about that?" Ellen asked.

Donna took a deep breath, wondering how honest she could be with Ellen, who had the reputation of telling Jack everything. She paused.

Ellen guessed why Donna hesitated. "I know it looks like I share everything with Jack. He likes to give that impression because it takes the attention away from what he picks up and guesses at. But I'd like for you to think about developing a trusting relationship with me. I can absolutely keep confidences, and I know peer coaching won't work if we can't be honest with each other. Besides, I would like to confide in you. I haven't had someone to really talk to since I was promoted a few years ago."

Donna searched Ellen's eyes for any sign of evasion, then sighed and started talking. "The reason it feels like I have been here three years is that in dog's years it has been three. The pressure is really intense, and I feel like no matter how hard I work or how late I stay, I can't make any progress. Working like a dog..." she trailed off.

"I can see that," Ellen said.

"You mean that my tongue is hanging out and that I am out of breath?" laughed Donna.

"No, that you are working lots of hours and trying to get things done."

"Yes, and the harder I work, and the more days, and nights, frankly, that go by, the more there is to do. I am concerned that our marketing message about Tech Environments isn't getting through, and I have started to wonder how much I will need to push to get a clearer sense from Jack about where we are headed. It's really hard to build a marketing plan and execute it when we aren't sure of our strategy. In the agency I worked at before, client strategy was pretty clear. Here it seems to depend on which day it is, and who's talking! There, I've said too much already."

"You probably didn't realize that is why you were hired—Jack is struggling right now with the company strategy, but he hasn't wanted to admit it. He didn't share that with you in the interview?" Ellen made this last statement in a questioning tone.

Donna answered quickly. "Absolutely not, because I wouldn't be the best person for the job of creating a business development strategy. I had very little client interaction at the agency, and I don't have much corporate experience. Oh dear, how am I going to make that happen?"

Ellen offered reassurance. "Don't worry, Donna. If we can make this team work, you will get help from everyone, including Jack—the guy who never needs help!"

"In a strange way I feel better at least knowing what you know about my role. I just can't get my feet under me, and every time I approach Jack, he says everything is fine. But it isn't."

They sat in silence for a moment.

"So how about you?" Donna asked. "What did you want to talk about?"

Ellen lowered her voice and said, "I'm concerned about my role, too. My job has devolved into Jack's 'Chief of Staff' rather than an officer position. If everyone has the same opinion you do—that I tell Jack everything and that I function like a highly paid assistant to him—that's not good. I am also concerned about everyone holding me responsible for teamwork on our team. How would I ever make that happen by myself? But for some reason I keep trying to solve all of the people problems."

Donna nodded sympathetically. "I don't know how you do what you do," she said.

In the lull that followed Ellen's confession, Donna glanced at her watch and saw that half the time was up for their peer coaching. "Oops, we better do what Jordan asked: discuss our strengths and our development areas. I think we already did a pretty good job of talking about our problems. You think going from there into our development goals and strengths is a good idea?"

"Sure," Ellen replied. "I'll start. My strengths as a leader are these: I am good at collaborating and building relationships. I am a good listener and a good coach. I deliver results and I am team oriented. What I need to develop is the ability to say no—to Jack—and to quit taking on everyone's problems. I guess I also need to be more strategic in what I do, rather than lurching from problem to problem."

"I can see your strengths showing up every day in what you do. How will you tackle saying no, and not trying to fix things that are out of your control?"

"I don't know," Ellen replied. "If I did, I'd be doing it."

Again, both of them were silent.

"For me," said Donna, "it's influence. I need to be able to influence Jack and the rest of the leadership team to focus on strategy and on our marketing message. I don't think the company will be successful if we don't. And I know my strengths are focusing, delivering, and executing. I am also pretty creative. But influence—that's something I really need to get better at."

"Well, I am influenced by you already. I know you work hard and you care about this company. You aren't a quitter. That counts for a lot around here."

40
TED AND ARUN SURPRISE EACH OTHER

If anyone was less pleased with their partner for peer coaching, neither Arun nor Ted could imagine it. Jordan must not know them very well if she was making this match!

"Well, I guess we need to get to work," Ted said as he closed the door to the small conference room firmly. "What did you decide your development goal was going to be?"

Arun glanced at Ted before answering. "I don't think you are going to like it much, but everyone else agrees with me. My goal is to get this team to be more innovative. We can never compete in the marketplace if we aren't getting new processes and products out there more quickly."

Ted quickly challenged Arun. "That sounds like the same thing you've been saying in all of our leadership team meetings. Jordan said our development goal has to be a personal one, something we know we need to get better at, or even something we need to stop doing. She definitely said it has to be a personal commitment." He stopped, looking at Arun with a mixture of irritation and challenge.

Arun didn't look back. Head down, he spoke quietly. "I didn't really realize that we were going to be sharing our personal goals with each other. I'm more comfortable keeping that to myself."

"Okay, Arun, now you've surprised me," Ted responded. "Do you mean to say you didn't hear everything Ellen and Jack have been saying about teamwork? How are we going to have a team if we aren't telling each other our goals?" At Arun's startled look, he finished more gently. "I mean, if we aren't going to take risks, how are we going to get any better? I don't know if I can stand to be here another two years as CFO if we are at each other's throats the way we have been these last few months."

Now it was Arun's turn to be surprised. "I didn't realize it actually bothered you, Ted. You always seem pretty sure of yourself and the way you do things."

Ted was quick to respond, "Yes, I know I seem that way. But to be honest, I am pretty concerned about all the transitions we are making and whether we'll make it through. In my thirteen years here, we've been through a lot. But this is the shakiest I've ever seen Jack, and the worst I've ever felt myself. I want to work two more years, but not if it's like this."

"I might be heading out the door with you when you leave," Arun replied. "It hasn't been a picnic for me, either. Maybe Jordan had a plan when she paired us up after all. I didn't realize we were both so dissatisfied." He and Ted looked across the conference table at each other, not sure of how to continue.

Arun spoke again, "Something you just said about us taking risks struck me. Usually you tell me I'm taking too many risks and spending too much money on new things. We argue about that all the time. What do you mean when you say we need to start taking some risks? That doesn't sound like you."

"Okay, I guess that means I'm going first with my goal. This might sound stupid to you, because risk taking comes easy for you, Arun. But it's never been my strong suit. Actually my risk aversion has often saved the day for Tech Environments. We got through the worst of the economic crisis because of how we had our loans and client agreements structured, and Jack has always been appreciative of my ability to protect us financially. As I think about retirement, though, I am realizing I have to get more comfortable with change. My development goal is to take one risk each day. I quantified it so I could easily track my progress."

Though Ted had been completely sincere as he said this, Arun burst into laughter. "I can't believe you put a number to it, Ted! That is hysterical. You are such a numbers guy! Let's see, with twelve company-wide holidays a year, that means you'll take 248 risks this year. I can't wait to see that."

"Actually," Ted said with a grin, "it's only 233 risks. I take three weeks of vacation."

They both burst into laughter, enjoying Ted's joke.

"Okay, well, since you shared yours, I'll share mine," Arun stated. "It's a bit embarrassing, but my goal is to not be so arrogant. I'm usually so sure that I know the right answer that it can be irritating to others. I believe it keeps my team from sharing more of their own ideas. Even more important, I think, is that it causes conflict on our leadership team, not just with you."

He added, "Jordan told me my goal shouldn't be framed as a negative, so she challenged me to state it more positively. Instead of having the goal of *not* being arrogant, I'm going to work on expressing appreciation. I read an article on Forbes.com that gratitude is an underutilized leadership strategy, and I think if I focus on appreciating others, it will keep me from thinking I'm always the one with the best ideas. I won't come across as so arrogant."[26]

Ted jotted down both their goals on his tablet and looked at them:

- Arun will express more appreciation.
- Ted will take at least one risk each day, a total of 233 a year.

"Okay, not bad. So we've got that part of our assignment done. How about your top three strengths?" Ted asked.

"Creativity. Courage. Confidence. Easy to remember with the three Cs. How about you?"

Ted added Arun's strengths to his document, and then glanced down again at his tablet. "My strengths are clarity, support, and competence.

Another couple of Cs, with an S thrown in the mix. No surprises there, I think. What do you think about the team's strengths?"

Arun reflected for a minute before answering. "It hasn't felt like we had many strengths recently. If you would have asked me a year ago, I might have said some of our strengths were stability, communication, and trust. Clearly all those are out the window now. With you leaving and Donna so new, and with Edgar in the Chief Risk Officer role, half our team is rolling on or rolling off. So stability is out the window."

"Hey, don't get rid of me so quickly," Ted cautioned. "I've still got two years left."

Arun laughed before continuing. "I just mean we don't have the stability we had a year ago because of all the changes. And maybe that's why our communication and trust are low too. But there I go being negative again. You asked me what our strengths are right now. I guess I think one strength is the talent we have on the team. We really do have some of the best talent in the technology industry in each of the roles on the leadership team. So we have that going for us. What do you think our strengths are?"

"I was actually going to say talent, too," Ted confessed. "I think it could be part of the problem, because we are all used to being the best and not so used to collaborating and taking a back seat. Maybe the other strength I am starting to see is openness. You know, I wasn't a fan of us spending the time or the money on this team coaching. But I couldn't come up with an alternative, and Jack insisted. Now I'm starting to see that Jack is being more open about his worries and that we could be more of a team. And if you and I, of all people, can be more open with each other, that makes me feel like there is hope after all."

Ted and Arun were startled by a knock on their door. Ellen poked her head in to say it was time for the group to gather briefly before ending their time today. "Who would have thought the two of you would be the ones who couldn't stop talking?" she said, amused.

41

THE CEO DOESN'T KNOW

It had been a week since their first team coaching session, and Jack was nervous. He was used to worrying, but nervous? That was new. He knew exactly what was making him anxious. In a few minutes he was planning to tell the team—his whole team—why he was worried, and the reason was about himself for a change.

Jack had tried to tell Edgar some of what was bothering him in their peer coaching. But Edgar still believed everything had an answer. It was the second meeting with Jordan that had done Jack in. Her question—"What is it you are hoping I don't ask you?"—unraveled everything. He squirmed with discomfort, thinking about their conversation. At first he tried to dodge her by not answering, but when he looked up and saw her steady gaze, well, that was it.

So he told her. All of it. That he just didn't know what to do anymore. The market was gobbling up the smaller-tier players, and his company was having trouble finding that sweet spot where customization mattered to clients, but not so much that they wanted to code themselves. Tech Environments had bet a lot on the new software release, but their strongest competitor had just put out a cloud-based offering, and they were getting all the attention now. Jack had always been proud of his strategic strength; now it felt hard to even identify it as one. Being decisive was another strength he'd always been able to count on, yet he was finding it much harder lately to make the big decisions.

Of course, one of the reasons it was harder had to do with the leaders not getting along, and Jack not feeling good about their functioning as a team. But Jordan had helped him see that he was not feeling confident or sure about himself. That's what Jack needed to reflect on and sort out.

He glanced at his watch. *Oh, great,* he thought, *only five more minutes. I am just going to tell them that I am not used to being unsure, that I don't know what to do, and that I need their help.* Sort of like the John Wooden saying Jordan shared with him: "It's what you learn after you know it all that counts."

Jack got up when he heard the voices of his team. *They sure sound lively,* he thought to himself.

TEAM COACHING, TAKE TWO

42

Ellen sat across from Jack, while Edgar and Donna sat on either side of him as they discussed that morning's *Wall Street Journal* article about outsourcing technology needs. Tech Environments had gotten a brief, relatively positive, mention along with speculation about where they were heading in their growth. Their main competitor had gotten slammed for lack of reliability of the cloud product they'd just introduced. The relief on Jack's team was palpable.

Jordan joined the group and pulled the door closed. "Ready to start?" At their nods, she said, "Let's do a two-word check-in to get a quick reading on how everyone's doing. Arun, why don't you start us off?"

"*Gloating. Happy.*" Arun stated.

"Two words is hard," said Donna. "Maybe *breathing*, and *anxious.*"

Jack concurred. "*Anxious* for me, too, and *open.*"

"I'll say *curious* and … I don't have a second word, I guess. Just *curious.*" Edgar stated.

"*Burdened* and *responsible*," Ellen offered.

"And for me, *status quo*," Ted added. "Everything is pretty much the same as always."

"What do you make of that range of check-ins?" inquired Jordan.

"What do *you* make of it?" responded Ted.

"I wonder if the team is ready to work together today or if some of the check-ins need exploring. Is there a question you want to ask anyone to clarify what's up for them?"

Donna looked directly at Ellen, "Can you say more about your check-in? *Burdened* and *responsible* sounds heavy. I knew I was anxious, but you surprised me with that."

Ellen answered slowly, without making eye contact with anyone, "Well, I have heard concerns recently, and they are actually about the leadership team here in this room. I am trying to figure out whether they are just complaints or a symptom of a bigger problem. And I am not really sure if this is the place to address them or not."

Everyone looked expectantly at Jordan. She responded to their unspoken question, "We can talk about whatever is most important here. And we had a plan for today to begin to look at the team as a whole: everyone's strengths and a leadership goal to set a foundation of trust and to find out what each of you wants to develop. What's the sense of the team about the best direction for us to go?"

Edgar spoke up. "I'm pretty direct, so I don't really want us tiptoeing around. If Ellen has a complaint about one of us, I hope we will be able to deal with it directly. If it's about me, I'd like to know."

"I'd like us to at least get our strengths and goals listed on the whiteboard before we go there," Jack said. "I know we all agreed we are willing to be open, but Jordan is right: we want to develop ourselves as a team that works effectively together. I think that probably starts with recognizing what we are good at."

"How do the rest of your feel?" Jordan asked. Based on the head nods and direct looks at Jack, she surmised that they wanted to talk about strengths and development goals first.

"Who wants to put these up on the whiteboard?" she asked.

"I will," said Jack, wanting to volunteer for a role he rarely played, in the spirit of mixing it up and being open.

After twenty minutes of sharing and clarifying, they had a chance to look at what Jack had written. Arun whistled. "Pretty impressive team. No wonder I'm on it."

"Yes, it looks like we have a lot of strengths," Jack said. "If I just looked at this list, I'd feel pretty good about our team. Our goals cover the whole

Ellen	Collaboration Rel—building Teamwork	Say No
Ted	Clarity Support Competence	Take 1 risk a day
Jack	Committed Decisive Competitive	Ask for help
Donna	Focus Execution Creativity	Influence other leaders
Edgar	Risk Reduction Directness Consistency	Grow Self— awareness
Arun	Creativity Courage Confidence	Express appreciation

gamut from self-awareness to asking for help. Some of them aren't as measurable as others, but it's good to know what everyone's working on going into this team coaching."

"Yes, no real surprises here," noted Ted. "Except for maybe Ellen's 'Say no.' Does this relate to what you were saying before, Ellen?"

Ellen spoke up. "I know you all wanted to hear about the concerns I mentioned, and I think they may fit in well here."

Everyone turned to Ellen. She spoke quickly, "As many of you know, I tend to feel responsible for all the leadership and people issues around here—and when engagement was up and things were going pretty well, I liked thinking that was my job. Now, though, I am realizing that we all must step up to the leadership issues here—they are not mine to solve. Since I am running the engagement focus groups, I have heard a lot of concerns these past few weeks from our people.

"The general feeling is that we are not working together as a team, that there is too much infighting over direction and resources, and that each of us has a sink-or-swim attitude about each other's areas and teams. I know this is hard to hear, but in some of the engagement focus groups, associates have said that that is why people are thinking about leaving, even in this iffy economy. They aren't sure we are heading the right direction and that we can make it the way we are—or really aren't—working together."

The team sat in silence, absorbing what they had just heard. Ellen looked over at Donna, who gave her a small smile of encouragement.

Jack spoke up, slowly and with frequent pauses. "I thank you, Ellen, for what you just said. I have been part of that problem, and I have wanted to step up and say so. It's been easy for me to let you be responsible for people while I worried about the important things like strategy and our future direction. But everything is coming together here in a way that really isn't working ... we have people who don't get along and don't collaborate—on this team and throughout the company—*and* we have some major strategy decisions that I cannot make alone. I need your help. Like I never have before. In order for you to help me, and help the company, we will need to pull together and forget about what's good for our departments and focus on what's good for the company. And maybe it starts with me recognizing that people are *not* less important than strategy and results."

As he looked out on his team's faces—some of them looked stunned, some looked guilty, others puzzled—Jack felt surprisingly confident. For the first time in several months he felt hopeful about the future.

"We're behind you, Jack," said Ted, finally breaking the silence. "Yes," agreed Edgar, Donna, and Ellen. "I know we can win in the marketplace," exclaimed Arun.

Jordan looked at the clock, and knew she needed to help the team close out.

"Jack, Ellen, thank you for your openness and willingness to say you need help. I think we have some great leadership here at Tech Environments. I know you have some key planning sessions coming up, too, so you might consider what Ellen shared and find ways to respond to the feedback by trying some new behaviors.

"Before we go, let's do a one-word check-out."

Not surprisingly, Jack and Ellen's word was the same: *relieved*. Ted's was *worried*, Arun's and Donna's was *hopeful*, and Edgar was still *curious*.

As everyone headed out, the mood was serious, and Jack noticed a look of determination on several faces. He wondered if this was a good sign or if he might have waited too long to address the issues on the leadership team. As Ellen headed out, she was wondering the same thing.

43
INVESTING IN TECHNOLOGY

Arun was running late, but he hoped that Donna and Ted would understand. He wasn't worried about the hardware vendor, Freddy, who was used to Arun being late. Arun's team was used to his lateness, too. Arun guessed that was part of what was perceived as arrogance: always being late when he could get away with it. *But no,* he thought, *I truly am busier than everyone else. Really.*

As Arun burst into the conference room, Ted looked up with a grimace. Arun knew that it ticked Ted off when anyone was late. *Hey,* he thought, *maybe that is the one risk Ted can take today—deciding not to be angry.* Arun hoped he hadn't used up all of Ted's patience.

Freddy was all smiles, as usual, and Donna looked serious, her typical outlook. Those members of the technology and financial staff who'd been invited to the meeting all looked noncommittal. "Let's get started!" said Arun.

"Finally," Ted barked. Freddy's smile wavered, and Donna looked up. A few raised eyebrows and anxious looks came from others. *Oh boy,* thought Arun.

About halfway through Freddy's presentation, Ted interrupted: "Just tell us how much this is going to cost."

Before Freddy could answer, Arun inserted, "There you go again, Ted." Donna looked deeply embarrassed, as did Freddy. There was an awkward silence around the conference room table.

"Seriously?" asked Arun. "Is cost all you care about? Don't you want to understand how we will use this investment?" Several technology team members nodded their agreement.

Ted suddenly noticed that their respective team members were sitting with each other, facing off across the table: technology on one side, finance on the other, with Donna and Freddy at either end. Maybe this was what Ellen was talking about. He knew immediately what he had to do.

Ted responded seriously, "Here is the thing you don't understand, Arun. I trust you, I really do. I think you have good judgment, and I think you have Tech Environments' best interests at heart. The only thing I don't trust is that you can get us the best deal. As CFO, that's my job."

Something shifted on Arun's face, and he actually seemed to relax. "Thank you, Ted. I appreciate your honesty. Let's give Freddy five more minutes to wrap it up and to make sure we all see what we might be buying here. You are leaving us the price quote today, right?"

Freddy nodded, and then he took them to the last few slides on design and functionality. Ted and Donna each asked a couple of questions. As Freddy packed up his briefcase, he offered to answer any other questions that came up. Donna quietly asked Arun and Ted to stay after the meeting, and everyone else filed out. Then, finally it was just Donna, Arun, and Ted again, with the price slide displayed on the screen.

"You know, I think you did a great job there of the good cop/bad cop routine," Donna said. "At first I was concerned about where things were going, but I really liked what you said, Ted. We have to trust each other and our respective expertise, *and* we have to do the jobs we were hired to do."

She paused and continued, "But that's where I am having some trouble—doing my job. I am not quite sure where we are going, and I still don't understand how decisions, including this one, are made around here. I can't really push our services if I don't know what we are planning."

Ted reassured Donna: "That's what we need to face in our next leadership team meeting when you present the marketing plan. Where are we going, and are we all aligned?" Arun nodded his head in agreement.

"That seems kind of backward to me: I develop a plan around a strategy that's not agreed upon, and we all argue about it," muttered Donna dryly.

"It's not usually like this, Donna," Ted answered. "But it is right now."

Pointing at the screen again, Ted brought them back to the meeting's focus. "Okay, let's get back to this price quote. Where do you think the padding is, Arun, based on your detailed understanding of the technology and this design?" asked Ted.

INVESTING IN PEOPLE

Patrick's new plan for developing leaders at all levels of the organization made sense to him and to his boss, Ellen. He looked over the slide with all the details.

LEADERSHIP DEVELOPMENT PLAN

- Career planning for the most junior people
- New supervisor training for recently hired or promoted managers
- Agile teams for innovation
- Leadership group coaching and stretch assignments for the high-potential managers
- Executive coaching and team coaching for the C-suite leaders

---

In addition, anyone could attend off-site training and conferences to further develop technically, with their manager's approval and as long as there was budget for travel. The whole plan looked pretty good, especially after Patrick inserted senior leadership team coaching into the plan when Jack unexpectedly added that initiative.

119

As he prepped for the meeting with the senior leaders, Patrick was pleased that Ellen was finally delegating more of the overall plan development and presentation responsibilities to him. He was proud that he'd stayed on top of the leadership development and talent literature and felt he had a pretty good level of expertise. He recognized that development was not just about training and skills development (what was referred to as "horizontal development") but also about helping leaders gain in self-awareness and consciously grow themselves (now known as "vertical development").[27]

Each person had to own his or her development, and be willing to recognize that the journey in personal growth was never complete. Not a comfortable place for any of them, not nearly as comfortable as straightforward skills development. But it was a different world now, and a good people development plan was critical. Though Ellen had not had much time to spend with him recently, Patrick knew that she felt good about the plan, too. Now they'd get to see if everyone else was on board. The fact that Jack had seen the value of group coaching was a good sign.

"Should we wait for Edgar?" Ellen asked as she looked at the clock.

Jack looked around, "I guess not. We need to get through this, and no one's heard from him. Let's go ahead. I'll IM him and his admin on the off chance that he's forgotten. Probably just got hung up. Please go ahead, Ellen."

At Ellen's nod, Patrick stood up and carefully went through all the details of the people plan. His presentation style was crisp and clear, so there weren't many questions. Even Edgar's arrival twenty minutes into the session had not seemed to interrupt Patrick's flow. "This plan offers a good balance of meeting individual and organizational needs," Patrick summarized. "And it's designed to put the accountability for development on each associate, which will ensure we don't become stagnant or complacent. We can attract and keep the right talent in place so we can keep innovating and growing."

Seeing that Patrick was done, Ted raised his hand. "This seems like a lot of money for soft skills," Ted observed. "Can't we ask managers to do more of the development so we can minimize the costs? Arun and his team are asking for technology changes, too, and Donna is agitating for us to up our marketing and business development budget. We simply don't have money for all of these things at once. Soft skills seem like something that can wait."

Though Ted's comments were stated respectfully, Patrick looked a little rattled. After a brief pause, however, Patrick referred Ted to one of the handouts on the cost per employee at each level of the organization, noting that the proposed costs were on par with industry standards. Jack jumped in. "It looks like Patrick's done his homework. I'm learning that the people development side of our business is just as critical as technology and strategy." Ted looked thoughtful, and made no further comment. Ellen smiled as Patrick asked for other questions.

Arun chimed in next. "I'm not so worried about the cost as about what kind of leadership culture we are creating here. What difference does it make to develop people if we don't have a culture where they can thrive? Right now, we are waiting to commit to new technologies. Soon we will be behind our competitors."

Donna broke in: "Arun, this is what we were talking about with Jordan—thinking of our own concerns rather than viewing the company as a whole. I know we have a strategy question on the table, but can we afford to ignore everything else? I think not." Because her comments were stated mildly, Arun seemed pacified.

Jack spoke up next and thanked everyone for participating, while smiling at Arun for backing down.

Then Jack asked, "How is this plan going to change our engagement scores?"

Ellen spoke this time. "I know I need to step up to solve our engagement scores, and I promise they will be better next year. But research shows that there is a strong connection between associate development and engagement, especially with millennials. Patrick, can you package some of the highlights of those studies and get that out to everyone?" Patrick nodded, and they started to leave the room.[28]

Jack tapped Edgar's shoulder as they got up. "Got a minute to talk?" Edgar looked uncomfortable but nodded and walked out with Jack.

As everyone else headed out the door, Ellen sat back down at the table with Patrick.

"Tough crew," he commented. "We have our work cut out for us. I liked Arun's comment about the leadership culture, even though he shows his hand again and again. You guys must have really gotten into being direct and honest with each other at your last team coaching for Donna to have spoken up like that. I really liked the way she made a tough point in a nice way."

"I agree," she responded. "We are all learning how to be better leaders for the whole company, not just for our roles. Were you surprised when Jack said that engagement was everyone's job? That came out, too, in the last team coaching."

"Sounds like you guys are getting a lot out of it, and it's beginning to show."

"Yes, thank goodness. On another note, Patrick, I want to tell you how much I appreciate the phenomenal job you did, with the plan and with keeping your cool about the questions. We make a good team."

"We do at that," Patrick smiled as they gathered their materials and headed back to their offices.

45
DONNA PRESENTS THE MARKETING PLAN

Ellen gave Donna an encouraging smile as she found her seat at the conference room table. Ellen had wanted to get to the meeting early to ask Donna what help she needed, but a last-minute phone call from Patrick meant she was delayed.

Donna looked worried, and Ellen guessed why. From their conversations, Ellen knew that Donna didn't like conflict, especially since she was new to the team, and that she wasn't happy being the instigator by presenting a marketing plan that would surely bring all their disagreements out in the open.

Donna had agonized about how to present a plan that no one agreed upon. Finally, she decided to spend more time on her analysis of the market and their competitors than she typically would. Their world was changing quickly, and she had some new data she felt would be helpful. Sharing that would at least give them all the same grounding. *Then let the arguments begin,* she thought ruefully. Ted was sure to argue against the massive infrastructure investment a cloud-based strategy shift would entail, and Arun would be absolutely insistent that it was the only way to proceed.

Both she and Ellen were beginning to understand what a huge gamble a strategy shift would be. In technology, the timing of your strategy was everything. Donna was curious about how Jack and Edgar would weigh in (both had seemed preoccupied lately). Nevertheless, it was clear that their market position was eroding to cloud-based services, and if they didn't change something soon, they might not be able to recover lost market share.

After she finished the market overview, Jack broke the silence that had descended on the room by complimenting her on how thoroughly she had explained the market data.

Donna thanked Jack, and then turned to the revenue analysis she had put together. She made eye contact with Ted as she began, "I know, Ted, that you always do a great job with revenue growth, margin analysis, and expense regression, so I decided to look at our revenue from a market-based view. Here is what I found."

They all looked up at the screen, which showed the numbers that led to Donna's conclusions: while gross revenues and margins were growing, that growth had obscured the fact that they weren't adding new accounts. Most of the growth was due to larger accounts that were growing through acquisition and, as a result, were buying more of Tech Environments' customized desktop software.

When those one-time revenue bumps were factored out, Tech Environments' revenue had actually declined year-over-year by 6 percent, and the rate of decline had been growing over the past several years, from a 2 percent decline, to 3 percent, to the current 6 percent. Projected out over three years, the numbers were alarming.

"If we lose just one of these accounts, we are in big trouble," said Donna. The room became very quiet. "And if their mergers and acquisitions activity slows, we are also in trouble."

Arun started to speak, but he glanced Ted's way and saw Ted give a small shake of his head. So Arun waited. As Arun's eyes followed Ted's, he was surprised to see everyone looking at Jack. Jack's eyes were down. The silence grew.

Finally Jack spoke up. "I'd like to adjourn this meeting and pick up the discussion in our team coaching later with Jordan." With that, he got up slowly and left the room.

46
ELLEN AND DONNA STEP UP THEIR GAME

"You are a rock star!" Ellen exclaimed when Donna showed up in her office fifteen minutes after the meeting where she had presented her marketing data. Donna grinned and ducked her head. Ellen went on, "You did exactly what needed to be done—you shared the data we needed to step forward into the future, and the way you presented it was courageous and brilliant!"

"I couldn't have done it without your help," she said. "I also bolstered my courage by remembering something Ted and Arun talked about when Freddy was here. As they say, 'No guts, no glory!'" exclaimed Donna.

"Well, welcome to Tech Environments! How did you know that was our motto?" They shared a laugh. Then, remembering how subdued Jack had been at the end of the market and account analysis, they got serious.

"If it's okay with you, Donna, I'd like to switch gears and talk about an issue I have," Ellen said. "I need your help. You got to see in our HR meeting with Patrick the way Jack holds me responsible for all the people issues around here. How am I going to deal with that?"

"You really want me to tell you what I saw?" asked Donna.

"Yes, I really do."

"I heard you step forward and ask to take that on, when you promised Jack you would make sure our engagement scores were better next year. It seemed like you took ownership, or you and Patrick did, even when you say you want all of us to own the people issues."

In the silence that followed, Donna asked Ellen, "What were you feeling when you made that promise about engagement scores to Jack?"

Ellen answered, "It felt great to make the promise, and I could feel a surge of energy and pride, but almost as soon as I said it, I felt really exhausted. Exhilarated for one second, exhausted for the rest of the year!"

As Donna looked at her kindly, Ellen went on, "I think I need to come clean with Jack. It kind of feels like I have been leading him on, based on wanting to feel important and have him believe—really believe—that it's right that I was promoted to Chief People Officer. I honestly believe I'm the right person for the role, but now I see that I set myself up to try to accomplish something that no one person could do. Patrick is great, as you could see. Still, I need Jack and all of you to recognize that if we don't all work on people and engagement, there is no way I, or anyone, can succeed in this role. No matter what promises I've made."

After a brief silence, Donna asked, "When will you have the conversation?"

"I need to think it through first," Ellen said. "I have to figure out what I am responsible for. And I need to be ready to explain that I was stepping out to prove myself by trying to accomplish the impossible. Wonder if we could talk more about this now, and maybe role-play a bit, like we do in team coaching, so I can get some practice?"

"Ho ho!" answered Donna. "I will have fun playing Jack. Let me try to get in his mindset for a few minutes so we can play it true to life."

"Thanks," said Ellen. "Maybe practicing will help make it real. I know I have to do this; I just don't want to."

"Yep," said Donna. "I know the feeling!"

47
JACK'S ONE-ON-ONE COACHING

Jordan arrived a few minutes early for her coaching session with Jack. He wasted no time in getting started.

"Jordan, I think I am beginning to get a clue about what's going on. In the last week or so, I've been in on, or heard about, several different high-level planning sessions that greatly impact the future of Tech Environments."

Jordan nodded.

Jack continued, "One meeting was a session with a vendor and Ted and Arun regarding a significant investment in new technology. You might have heard about that one, as there was some tension among our leaders that was obvious to the vendor, and to their respective teams."

When Jordan didn't respond, Jack went on, "And the other session was a focus on our market analysis, both the importance of generating new business and the dire situation we are in if we don't. As one of our newest team members, Donna did a phenomenal job of taking a fresh look at our business model and markets to see how we need to more strategically market to clients. She shared some challenges that, frankly, surprised most of us on the leadership team. We've had our heads in the sand. I ended that session a little prematurely when I realized that I needed some reflection time, and an objective ear, to put my thoughts together before I meet with the team again."

"Well, I can definitely offer an objective ear, Jack. What else do you want to walk away with today?"

"I think I understand more now about why I've been feeling so unsure of myself. I'd like to talk that through and see if you think I'm on target.

Then I'd like to figure out how to actually put my plan of asking for help into action with the executive team." He stopped, appearing deep in thought.

"Is there something else?" Jordan prompted him.

"Yes, there is," Jack said. "It's clear that even though we are starting to do some good work in our peer coaching, and with the team as a whole, that we probably don't have as much time as we thought. We really are in crisis, and whatever plan we create has to have some short-term positive impact if we are to have any hope of Tech Environments being around for the long term."

"Sounds serious," Jordan agreed. "Where do you want to start?"

Jack spent the next fifteen minutes outlining some of the dots that had started connecting for him in the recent meetings. Jordan listened carefully and didn't interrupt. Finally, Jack paused and looked at her expectantly.

"Okay, Jack, would you like for me to share what I'm hearing?"

As Jack nodded, she began. "You were aware that you needed new blood on your leadership team; that's why you hired Donna and promoted Edgar. Having them on the team has made some of the team's bad habits obvious."

"Yes, we don't listen to each other. We just push our own views instead of learning from each other. I tend to focus solely on work and don't have much of a work-life balance, which sets a poor example for the team. We have a lot of stress and we don't manage it well. None of us is taking regular time to reflect on strategy. Another issue is that I don't ask about team members' personal lives and how those are affecting their work. As a leader, I would say that I've taken my team for granted and rarely let them know how much I respect and admire their work. Our bad habits have led to some pretty siloed ways of doing things. The fragmentation has contributed to my own feeling that I don't have control or a cohesive strategy. We are six people, not a united team."

Jordan nodded. "Did I also hear that you think you and Ellen have gotten too comfortable with each other and that this needs to change? As

128

awkward as Arun is in challenging you, it sounds like you've gotten value from his honest and direct feedback."

Jack nodded his agreement. "Yes, Ellen does a great job, but she doesn't really confront me about my leadership flaws. I need that. Arun can be such a one-note guy that it's easy to tune him out."

"So what about the threats to Tech Environments? You indicated they are more immediate than you realized."

Jack continued, "You know, Jordan, even though some of our associate engagement issues bother me, what really concerns me is the leadership team. Just when I need them to step up and view the concerns of the whole company as the most important thing, everyone seems to be hunkered down and focusing on their own areas. This tough strategic turning point will require a lot more out of all of us, just when we seem to be on our knees. Our competition has caught up."

"Are *you* hunkered down?"

Jack's face reddened as he realized that had also been his response to the problems.

"What are you going to do?" asked Jordan.

"Ask for help. I need to get the team to see what I see and to jump in with both feet before it's too late."

"So what approach are you planning to take with them?" Jordan persisted.

"I'm going to put the people first," Jack responded. "Call out the strengths of each team member and what they've accomplished. Then I'm going to tell them we'll need every bit of their talents to get through what's facing us. I can't do it alone."

"Anything else?"

"I think that's a start. I'm more optimistic than I was walking in here. Thanks for the ear."

"Any time," Jordan smiled.

48

TEAM COACHING— WAKE-UP CALL

The energy in the room was not nearly as positive as it had been for their last team coaching, Ellen noted as she grabbed a seat in the circle. Jack made eye contact with her, and she felt like he'd just read her mind. *The good, and bad, of working together for so long,* she thought.

When they'd all settled into their seats, Jordan surprised them by asking them to start by sharing how they'd slept the night before. They always had some kind of check-in question, but they'd never had this one.

"That's a strange question, don't you think?" Ted said. "Pretty personal."

Jordan responded calmly, "Yes, it is. I think we need to start with the personal. And, of course, this team coaching belongs to you, so if you want to suggest another way to connect with each other, please offer one."

Ted smiled. "It's helpful to know why you do what you do, and I'm willing to give this a try. I'm actually learning a lot. In the spirit of my goal of taking one risk a day, I've even tried some of your approach with my own team—like your two-word check-in and one-word check-out—fascinating way to build awareness and teamwork."

Jordan nodded. "Great job linking our sessions here with opportunities to practice with your team." Looking around the circle, she inquired, "Who'd like to get us started?"

"I will," responded Donna. "I actually slept well last night. Got out of here around 7:30, which is good for me, and had dinner with a friend. We didn't talk about work at all, and I slept like a baby."

"Not me," Arun followed. "I was pretty bothered by your presentation of our market issues. Maybe you have had more time to get familiar with it and know what we can do about it, but right now I'm worried. And tired. And can't think well. You know, I read a leadership blog just this week that if we don't get enough sleep, our brains can't wash away all the gunk so we can think well the next day.[29] That's how I feel: worried, tired, and fuzzy."

"I woke up in the middle of the night, too," said Edgar. "That was a pretty grim market analysis, and whatever we do or don't do will increase risk around here. That keeps me up at night."

"I couldn't get to sleep either," said Ellen. "Like Arun and Edgar, I'm pretty worried—not just about our external issues but the ones internal to the organization, including challenges on this team. Once I got to sleep, though, I didn't wake up until my alarm went off this morning. I was glad we had this meeting scheduled today so we could talk more."

Ted jumped in next, "I always sleep pretty well, and last night was no exception. I can usually manage to turn off my brain and relax at night."

"That leaves me," Jack said. "I slept well last night for the first time in a long time. I think I am starting to see some things differently on our team and in our company. I'd like to share a little more and ask for your help."

Everyone nodded and waited expectantly.

"I've come to the conclusion that Tech Environments is dying a slow death," Jack began. "I'm not saying this to panic you, just to share what I'm seeing. And actually, saying that was even softening it a little. Let me be perfectly honest: I believe that Tech Environments is dying and not slowly. When you look at all the problems we have both inside the organization and in our market, I'd say we won't be around this time next year unless we fix them." Jack deliberately made eye contact with each person. "I need to know if you all are willing to do what it takes. I need your help. Hell, we all need one another's help."

No one said anything.

"What are you asking?" Jordan prompted Jack.

"I'm asking that we all own the solution. A few years ago I read *The Five Dysfunctions of a Team,* and I remember being surprised at Lencioni believing that the foundation of effective team functioning was trust.[30] That seemed too basic to me, too soft for the business we are in. Now I see that part of why the six of us don't work effectively as a leadership team is that we don't know each other as people, much less trust each other. The conversation we just had about how we slept last night is more personal information than I've heard from any of you in a while. So I'm asking us to build trust first, but again, I don't think we have much time, and I'm not sure how we can do it that fast."

"Maybe we don't have as far to go as you think, Jack," Ted responded. Then he went on, "I suspect most of us would like to have more of a personal connection with each other. We spend a lot of time together. I believe we'd be a lot less likely to only pay attention to our own agendas if we actually felt some degree of caring for one another. I'm surprised to hear myself saying that, but then I've found it pretty eye opening to see that getting to know each other better has made it so much easier for Arun and me to see each other's perspectives when it comes to technology expenditures."

Donna and Jack both nodded, but no one seemed to know where to go next.

"Let's take a step back for a minute from this conversation. What do you notice about this team right now?" Jordan asked, reminding them of a strategy they'd learned in their coaching—observing and noticing without moving immediately to take action.

"I notice we're having a serious discussion, but we're not arguing," Donna commented. "And that makes it much easier for me to listen."

"Everyone's engaged," Arun said. "Even those who haven't said much are clearly present. I haven't seen anyone pull out their phone to answer a text in a long time. I was probably the worst one on that, actually."

"Yes, I notice that we are all committed to taking the time to be here together, or in our peer coaching or individual coaching. It has helped me see the necessity of taking time to reflect, listen, and talk. Not sure how I forgot that, given my role here. But like all of us, I've been running around putting out one fire after another for a long time," Ellen declared. "And I guess that makes me wonder: How are we going to change that habit here at Tech Environments? It's part of our culture to multitask, same-time message, act fast, and pay no attention to each other."

WHAT'S UP WITH EDGAR?

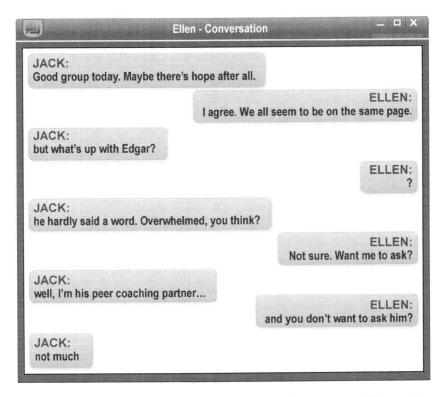

Ellen heard a tapping at her door and looked up to see Edgar. "Just a minute," she called.

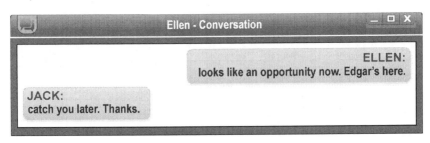

Ellen turned away from her desk and toward Edgar, "What's up? I noticed you were quiet in group."

Turning to close the door behind him, Edgar sat down. "I've got a problem, Ellen, and I'm hoping you can tell me what to do."

"An issue with your team?" Ellen asked. "Still having a hard time with resistance?"

"No, it's not that. It's my son, Josh. The other day when I was late to the presentation it was because I got a call from his school. Josh told another kid that he swallowed a handful of pills. His friend was worried and reported it. Long story, but they had to take him to the ER and pump his stomach. They got him there quick, and he should be fine, but we could have lost him. I can't get it out of my mind. It was pretty frightening for my wife and me. And I don't understand what is going on with Josh."

"How is Josh now?"

"He's home, and we've been trying to get him some help. I feel like I am being pulled in two directions. I didn't go to the hospital the other day, and I know I should have. But I was late to the meeting anyway, and I couldn't concentrate very well when I was here."

He sighed, and then added, "I'm not handling this promotion to Chief Risk Officer as well as I'd like. It should have been clear to me that I needed to be with my family at a time like that, but I'm so concerned about mastering everything and proving myself in this role that I couldn't see it. That's not who I want to be as a father, or a husband. I'm not sure where that leaves me."

"Do you know what's going on with Josh, why he did that?"

"We only know a little right now. Apparently he's being bullied at school, and they've been pretty nasty. He hasn't said much yet. To be honest, I think he was worried we'd be angry with him, or disappointed. I guess we've always made such a big deal about him being the big brother and how his sister looks up to him ... I think he felt like he should be able to handle it himself."

Ellen nodded sympathetically. "I can hear that being responsible is big for you both. You know we have an Employee Assistance Program here to help employees in situations like this?"

"Yeah, I thought about the EAP. Are they good? Could they help Josh and the rest of the family?"

"Yes, I'm sure they could. I'll get you a referral, and they should be able to get you seen today if that works for you," Ellen replied.

"Thanks, Ellen. That's huge for me." Edgar looked relieved. "Listen, I don't want to put you in the position of having to tell Jack. I know that sort of thing can be hard for you. Tomorrow I'll share with him what's going on."

"That's great, Edgar. And I hope everything goes well with the counselor today. Thanks for trusting me and sharing this. Please let me know how I can support you through this."

50
JACK AND EDGAR

Edgar was hurrying to Jack's office when Jack came barreling around the corner from the executive conference room.

"Oh, I was hoping to catch you, Jack. Do you have a few minutes?" Edgar sounded anxious.

A few minutes was the last thing that Jack had, and on top of that, he really didn't want to talk to Edgar. He knew he had to say yes, though, so he did. "Sure, Edgar. Will you head on into my office and wait for me for just a minute?"

When he got back to his office, Jack saw that Edgar was still standing around, awkwardly hovering near a chair. "Please, have a seat Edgar," suggested Jack, who pulled out a chair and made a point to seat himself next to Edgar instead of behind his desk.

Edgar began before Jack had fully taken his seat. "Jack, I'm sorry to dump this on you, with everything else, but I can't keep on going the way things are, and I felt you needed to know as soon as I knew that."

"Well, of course, Edgar. Tell me what's going on." A million reasons why Edgar would say that were racing through Jack's mind, but none of them were what Edgar was actually telling him. Jack tuned back in.

"…took the pills and had to have his stomach pumped. Josh is being bullied, and it's been going on for a while, and I never knew. I really haven't been there for my son, or my wife, and probably not for my daughter either. And now it's clear to me that I have to be there. I don't think this will wait—or should wait. And I don't see how I can continue on here at work as distracted and upset as I am."

"Of course, Edgar. How is Josh now?"

137

After Edgar explained, Jack went on to say, "Please, just plan to take the next few weeks or even the next month off, and we can look at things then. They will look different after a little time. That I do know."

The two men sat in silence for a few moments. Edgar went on to tell Jack about EAP, and Jack agreed that it was a good place to start.

"I just want you to know that anything you need, anything at all, you can come to me. This is serious business, Edgar. And you are right: your family needs you. Tech Environments has to come second right now."

Jack could see the emotion welling up in Edgar's eyes. Edgar stood up and held out his hand to Jack. "I really appreciate your support." Jack reached over and gave Edgar a tentative pat on his shoulder, regretting that they weren't closer, but glad that Edgar seemed to feel supported. What a terrible thing he was dealing with.

Before Edgar left, Jack made him promise to keep in touch about Josh and his family—but not about work. He made it clear that Edgar was to stop thinking about Tech Environments totally.

After Edgar left, Jack took a deep breath. *Boy,* he thought to himself, *that sure puts it all in perspective.*

51
THE TEAM MOVES FORWARD

Jack and the team met that afternoon. Everyone got quiet when they noticed Edgar's empty seat at the conference room table. News had traveled fast, because Edgar personally shared what had happened to his son with Arun, Donna, and Ted. He told them that he didn't want them to misunderstand why he was taking a leave of absence. After calling the EAP, he and Ellen and Jack had spoken again, and Edgar said that that was what he wanted—to take at least a three-month leave for personal reasons. Then he packed his briefcase with personal items from his office and left.

Arun spoke up first. "I feel like I really don't know Edgar that well—I have always treated him as the other guy who said no—like my friend Ted, here, but for a different reason—legal, not financial. I feel bad about what happened to his son, and I really feel bad for him. I can see how being here all the time keeps you from seeing your family. I think we all know that." Arun's tone was somber and his normally animated face was still.

Donna agreed. "This gives us all a chance to figure out what's most important."

Ellen was quiet, lost in thought.

"Well, I know why I'm here instead of anywhere else," Ted said. "I am here because I want to make a difference. I want to get this company back on track so I can retire happily. And I want to be here with all of you— even you, Arun."

They all looked startled by what they were hearing.

Donna recovered first, saying, "That's right, Ted. We have a job to do here, and like you, I am beginning to like working with you guys. We have struggled lately, and it hasn't been easy for any of us, but if each of us keeps looking out for the rest, we can hold it together. Hold it together long enough to move the company in the right direction."

This was a long speech for Donna. Everyone looked at Ellen and Jack, who both started to speak at once. Jack deferred, and Ellen spoke, "I think we have a choice here—we can work together or fall apart. I have put too much into this company to want to see it fall apart."

"Well put, Ellen. You know I always agree with you, and this time I really do," Jack said earnestly, while everyone else laughed. "Seriously, guys, I think we can do it, but it's going to take some more humility, some more hard work, and some more helping each other to pull this off. We have to get TE out of the ditch, and I know we can. I am really proud to work with such a great team of leaders, and I am really proud to serve as your leader."

"Do we need to take a vote?" asked Arun.

"It doesn't seem like it," boomed Ted.

"Okay, then," said Jack, "Let's decide how we are going to cover for Edgar, and let's decide how we are going to move forward on our cloud strategy. It's time—maybe past time—to make a decision. Let's make one together today."

EPILOGUE
One Year Later

It's just like old times, thought Jack, with everyone chattering as they came into the room. But not quite, he realized, because Ellen was gone, and so was Edgar. Still, they had a solid core of the same team. Donna had stayed on despite her rocky arrival during an iffy time for the company. Arun had taken over as both COO and CTO, reflecting his expanded role in the migration of Tech Environments' operations and technology platform from desktop to cloud.

And since Jack had promoted Patrick to an executive role—though not a C-level job; it was too early for that—the people part of their work had continued to thrive. Ellen had trained him well.

Edgar had been surprisingly hard to replace, and it had been a shock to Jack that he had left permanently. But as Jack knew from his own experience, personal issues trump business issues once they become serious, and Edgar's certainly were. The fear of losing a child has a way of making priorities clear, and Jack was glad Edgar had made the choice to put family first. Edgar's son Josh was thriving at the new school in the community they had moved to, and Tech Environments' "new Edgar"—a woman named Lynn—seemed like a good hire.

Ellen's departure had been the biggest bombshell, but frankly she seemed to have outgrown her role. Once everyone started taking responsibility for developing themselves and the leaders in their departments, Ellen had been ready for a bigger role, bigger than what Jack could provide at Tech Environments. She was lured away by the CEO of a much larger publicly held company who heard her speak at a Technology Leadership Conference. Just like that, they made her an offer she couldn't refuse, and Jack didn't blame her for leaving. She had always felt like his chief of staff, even though they both tried to break themselves of the habit of interacting that way. He wished her well.

Bringing himself back to the present, Jack noticed that everyone was seated, and he started their meeting, "Let's take a minute to reflect on the past year—the good, the bad, and what we've learned. And let's talk about the one thing we want to accomplish this coming year."

"I would like to go first," spoke up Arun. "For me, the good has been forging a stronger relationship with Ted and with Donna, so we were able to work together to implement this big initiative at Tech Environments. The good has also been expanded responsibilities, which I am very much able to carry out." This last remark was delivered emphatically by Arun and was met with smiles from Ted and Donna.

Arun went on. "The bad has been my attitude of knowing everything, and I have worked on that, and I can now admit there are some things I do not know. In the new year, I want to learn those things, and I want to keep working on developing a sense of humility to balance my confidence. My team will appreciate my not being a know-it-all. I trust that my colleagues Ted and Donna will keep helping me with that. At least, I hope so."

Ted picked up when Arun finished. "For me, the good has been feeling like I am more part of the decision making of the business, not just the 'always say no' CFO. I appreciate everyone helping me contribute in a broader way and supporting my goal to take more risks. I'd like to keep growing my role and continue to feel a valued part of the team. So the best way to get me to retire is to give me the cold shoulder!" They all laughed as Jack made a motion to move his chair away from Ted.

Ted went on. "Next year I would like to continue to partner with Donna to keep looking at our business model in new ways, not just holding down expenses, but understanding how the financials can help us make a difference in the market."

"I'll agree to that," said Donna, "because it fits in with my goal to deepen my knowledge of Tech Environments and to continue my shift away from just being a marketing expert to being a technology, market, and marketing expert. It was hard coming to Tech Environments last year and thinking the job would be straightforward. The bad part for me was learning to be confrontational when necessary; that's not my style. But I've learned a lot from the experience, and disagreeing with others has been easier than I had imagined."

Everyone laughed when Arun said, "That's how I find it: easy."

Patrick spoke up next and offered his thoughts. "I am happy to be part of the leadership team, and it's great to see how focused we all are on teamwork, collaboration, and helping each other grow. That's my goal—that we can be even better leaders a year from now than we are now, including me."

Lynn chimed in. "That works for me, as well as Donna's goal of learning more about the company. I am going to depend on all of you to help me do both of those things. I knew when I interviewed here with each of you that you had a strong team culture—that's what attracted me to Tech Environments."

Everyone looked at Jack to see what he would say. He took a moment to compose his thoughts and get his emotions in check. "You all have stepped up tremendously in the past year, and I have needed you to. We could only accomplish what we had to by working together. For a bit I felt like I had lost my way, but you helped me find the path forward. I think that we have a bright future and we can all be proud of how we have made that happen!" Jack raised his coffee mug and toasted them all: "Better days!"

"Hear, hear! Better days," the chorus of voices chimed in.

As everyone left the conference room, Jack remained seated and reflected. It was hard to believe it was just a year ago when he and Ellen talked about whether they could get the team back on track and how team coaching might help. It was pretty amazing to Jack how far they had come. In some ways that conversation with Ellen seemed like it had happened ten minutes ago, and in other ways—maybe in dog years, ha!—it seemed like it had happened long ago. *Yes,* he thought to himself, *better days indeed!*

ABOUT THE AUTHORS

ANN V. DEATON, PHD, PCC

After her first career in health care, Ann earned her leadership coaching certification from the Newfield Network in 2003. She founded DaVinci Resources to focus on coaching in health care in 2003 and joined the Bounce Collective leadership development in 2009. In her work in health care, corporate, and not-for-profit organizations, Ann coaches individuals, teams, and groups experiencing significant change and growth. Her favorite approaches include visual imagery, polarities management, and assessments. Ann earned her doctorate in Clinical Psychology, with specialization in health and neuropsychology, and has always appreciated the power of groups, both as a psychologist doing group therapy early in her career and for the past decade as a coach working with groups and teams. Ann enjoys having a ripple effect in the world through serving on the faculty at The University of Texas at Dallas coach training program and Virginia Commonwealth University's School of Business.

Ann can be reached at ann@bounceleadership.com; www.bounceleadership.com or www.beingcoached.com; or 804.955.4926.

HOLLY WILLIAMS, MBA, PCC

Holly's background includes leadership in a Fortune 50 technology firm, as well as setting up business training programs for a Virginia community college and business development for a tech firm. For over 15 years, her company, MAGUS Group Coaching, has coached executives and leaders to develop their leadership capacity in business and government. She took her MBA at George Washington University, completed the Georgetown coaching program in 2006, and joined its faculty in 2011. She coaches in financial services such as Capital One, Freddie Mac, National Cooperative Bank, and SWIFT. Besides group and team coaching, her current interests include narrative intelligence (archetypes) and personal branding, and adult development theory.

Holly can be reached at holly.williams@magusgroup.com; www.magusgroup.com; www.beingcoached.com; or 540.349.3086

KATE EBNER INTERVIEWS THE AUTHORS

Kate Ebner is the founder of Nebo and the host of *Visionary Leader, Extraordinary Life* on VoiceAmerica Business. She interviewed Ann Deaton and Holly Williams on February 7, 2014, to go behind the scenes of *Being Coached*. The interview is reproduced here as an opportunity for readers to catch a glimpse of the authors' thinking and goals in writing this book. Much like the book itself, this interview has a casual style that reflects the conversation that took place and the questions and responses that naturally came up for the three interview participants.

Legend of names: KE = Kate Ebner, HW = Holly Williams, AD = Ann Deaton

KE: You have written a new book about group coaching. Let's start by telling us about the impetus for writing this book. Holly, why don't you take this one?

HW: Group coaching is so powerful when people develop in a community, support each other in the process, and the coach's role is very light. The fingerprint—the touch—is light from the coach because there is so much going on amongst the leaders. I love to do this group coaching work and really wanted to find a way to get the story out about what it is, how it works, and how powerful it can be. Ann and I have known each other for a while and, of all the people who do group coaching, Ann, like me, really loves it.

KE: Ann, when might an organization reach for group or team coaching versus individual coaching?

146

AD: Individual coaching has become familiar to most organizations, and they've gotten comfortable using coaching and even seeing it as a perk for their leaders. Group and team coaching is less familiar, but the exciting thing about this approach is that it creates a fabric within the organization that is there long after the coach leaves. I find organizations look to group coaching when they want to give people an opportunity to look at their relationships with each other and strengthen their teamwork. Team coaching enables people to improve the strength of their team working relationships while being coached—and perhaps give each other feedback in a way they had never learned before nor taken the risk to do. Group coaching provides a chance for those who don't interact with each other regularly in the organization to work together across departmental function lines and see into each other's world a bit. It's just amazingly powerful.

KE: It sounds like two of the great benefits of group coaching are first, that it is a way to create a lasting circle of support within an organization as people learn how to be a group while learning together, and second, that the benefits last long beyond when the coach is present. The result of group coaching is a group who cares about each other and knows how to support each other. Group coaching is a great way to build community and capacity within the organization even among leaders who don't necessarily have reasons to work together day-to-day. Is that right?

AD: That's absolutely true. Group coaching builds community and capacity.

HW: I'd like to add that bigger organizations are looking for a way to differentially invest in leaders, develop leaders deep down in the organization that typically might be "underserved" by a coaching opportunity or a leadership development opportunity. I've found that group coaching programs can be put together with that in mind and, sometimes, organized with certain groups around a perceived need to develop more in one area or another—say, leadership presence, or communication skills, or influence skills. It's really a great opportunity to get coaching seeded in the organization before leaders become executives and might have greater access to coaching.

KE: Is group coaching an economical way to develop a group of leaders who are coming along in an organization, who might not be served by coaching otherwise?

HW: Absolutely.

AD: Kate, that's often what the impetus is: *We can't afford to invest in all of these leaders.* Group coaching offers a way to invest in them that's more affordable. That might actually be the organization's initial attraction to the concept—and then the unexpected gift of group coaching is: *Wow, that not only was a great way to invest in these individuals, but it was probably the exact right way to invest.* Not only are the leaders developing as individuals, they are also developing their networks, their ability to relate, and getting opportunities to practice leadership skills while experiencing coaching.

KE: Are there many people out there doing group coaching? Is this a new trend?

HW: We'd love to hear from more people who are doing group coaching. We want to connect with other coaches and with other HR leaders, people who are interested in group coaching, and who are actually doing group coaching. It's still a pretty new concept, and I think it calls for some additional skills on the part of the coach. Coaches may or may not want to develop the skills and competencies needed for group coaching. Coaching has an improvisational nature. Coaching happens in the moment and, as it happens, you don't really know moment to moment what's going to happen next. As a coach, you are supporting the conversation and the energy and direction of the clients. Well, when you have several people in the room it becomes, potentially, even more of an improvisation and even more "uncontrollable." Some coaches may be interested in being trained in the advanced improvisational skills that group coaching requires, while others may be more comfortable working one-on-one.

KE: For coaches, group coaching offers a wonderful new set of skills and processes to bring to client organizations. Having read your book and considered the case studies, one of the things I enjoyed is the friendly, accessible storytelling that you do that really brings the group coaching process to life for the reader.

In the book, you're using different kinds of examples. There's one example where you're working with a group of middle managers, and the group coach is helping these middle managers become a supportive group. My question is, Ann, for you: is group coaching equally effective for middle managers as for senior groups? And can you say a little about who benefits most if there is a difference?

AD: I think it is a different experience for senior managers versus mid-level managers or even emerging leaders. There are many commonalities in the struggles that we have as human beings. We all want to find meaning in the work that we do. We are all trying to find that right harmony between our work lives and our personal lives. When you're working with emerging leaders or middle managers, they are really trying to figure out how to do this, often for the first time as mature leaders. Watching each other work on this and seeing each other's successes takes away a fair amount of the fear. Seeing other people being successful and addressing their challenges is inspiring and energizing.

For more senior leaders, often what is lacking is a chance to be vulnerable with other leaders. They may be at a more confident stage of their careers and more comfortable with leading, but they don't have many places where they can actually be vulnerable and unsure of themselves. Group coaching can provide that opportunity for leaders at all levels, the opportunity to not know the answers and to trust that they can find those answers in a supportive and challenging context. For more experienced leaders, group coaching offers a rare place where they can get to do that.

KE: In the book, you write about trust and how it develops through group coaching. Holly, is trust a byproduct of group coaching?

HW: Trust is the foundation, to me, of almost all human interactions that go beyond transactions. In the coach/leader relationship, trust is absolutely critical, and that translates into any kind of coaching that we do. When we come in as group coaches, or team coaches, we must be able to form those bonds of trust individually with each leader and then collectively with the group. We provide a model to learn from and then open up that circle of trust to co-create a learning community. Trust is a really critical part of the coaching process.

KE: It can be hard to come by. I think as people work together in organizational life, there are many challenges, internal conflicts, or even friction between one function and another. In your book, you tell a great story about a senior leadership team that really learns to move beyond those kinds of tensions into a deeper-level relationship as a result of the group coaching. How does a group coach create safety so that trust can happen? What kinds of things does the group coach pay attention to or put into place, Ann?

AD: Coaches do this in very simple ways that they may not even be aware of. For example, by starting groups on time and asking everyone to make a commitment to be there every time. By ending on time. By always creating a way for people to check in and share how they are as they come in that day. And by inviting people to talk about what has "landed" with them when they leave the group at the end of the coaching session. Simple things like these structures enable people to gain a level of predictability and consistency: we're always going to start on time, I'm always going to have a chance to share what's up for me, and I'm always going to have a chance to say what I specifically am taking away from this interaction. So, simple structures create safety and build trust.

Also, people begin to recognize that we *will* differ, and *how* we differ is going to either make or break our relationships. We can choose to be different in ways that demonstrate respect for what the other brings—and also lets us share our own voice with the coach's support. We see that we are all right and they are also all right. Different voices, different ways of seeing all have a place in the group. That's an amazing experience. Many times in daily business, we have deadlines and we're trying to accomplish something; we're trying to cut to the chase and come to a decision. We forget that there can be multiple right answers. Sometimes, the coach must just let the group do its work and stand by to observe that people are challenging each other in respectful ways and caring ways that build trust. Profound differences don't create destructive conflict in a group coaching environment.

HW: I'd like to bring up something that we haven't talked about yet but fits into this conversation really well, and that's the work that leaders do in between their group coaching sessions. This work is done in pairs or triads. We use peer coaching quite a bit in both the team coaching and the group coaching processes. So, you know, in group coaching, a lot of work—most of the work—happens when the coach isn't even there.

KE: As I was reading your book, the characters in the book—who seem very true-to-life to me—were having insights when they weren't in the group but actually driving home, or in preparation for a meeting they were remembering things that they learned in the group coaching. They were able to access something important, distinctions about leadership their group coaching had taught them.

Holly, could you just describe for a moment the process of group coaching, so that if someone were learning about group coaching for the first time and wanted to hire a group coach, they would know what to expect the process to look like?

HW: There is a limit to the number of people who can work comfortably within a group. We've worked with different sizes, and I would say between eight and twelve people is a good-sized group. Twelve is typically the maximum. You can go with fewer than eight, but it's nice to have lots of energy in the room.

As far as the process of engaging group coaching, I would begin by trying to understand what the client is looking for and making sure that coaching really is the right developmental tool. Once I've established that and figured out what the goals are, then the next step is for the client to choose participants. You should have a good mix of people that is representative of the type of leaders the organization wants to invest in, especially if this is a pilot. First, choose participants, and then get schedules sorted out. We also like to do some individual coaching within the group coaching. So, setting up all the schedules and making sure that we can meet individually before the first group session with everyone to get some sense of what their strengths are as leaders, where they think they'd like to develop, how it is they're feeling about being in group coaching is very helpful. I want to make sure that they understand coaching and learn about their previous coaching experiences. As a coach, I want to have that individual connection with each person before we get to the first group.

I think the other thing to figure out: Is this a four-month program? Six-month program? What are the drivers, both in terms of goals at the end and economics that would help us structure a program that is going to meet the needs of the client?

AD: One thing I'd add to that, Kate, is from the get-go to have a conversation with the client about confidentiality. I think this is one of those things that we, as coaches, don't always think about sharing with clients early on, yet it is part of what creates trust and safety. The conversation with the organizational sponsor or whomever the champion of the coaching is ensures that we know the goals for what they want to see the group accomplish. That helps reinforce that the individuals in the group are actually going to be creating their own leadership goals. It will be up to participants to communicate with their managers and with the organization. The organization will see the results of the coaching work, and the coach will share in general what's happening in the coaching, but not specifics or personal information. That's going to be up to the individuals involved. As coaches, we must make sure that the organization understands the confidentiality issues. This is part of how we set things up to ensure that the group coaching is as powerful as it can be.

KE: Let's take the question of process from another angle: the perspective of the people participating. Can you give us a sense of how it works for the participants, both in the session and outside of the session? Holly?

HW: Typically the group coaching programs that I do are six sessions: six group sessions over four months. That's about one every three weeks. The group sessions are usually a couple of hours long. Folded into that several-month period are also three one-on-one sessions with the executive coach.

KE: So each individual gets a one-on-one session?

HW: Yes. Each person gets three hours of one-on-one time. The first individual session, as I mentioned earlier, takes place before the group starts. The second is in the middle, right between sessions three and four, ideally. Then the last one is after all the group sessions are completed. At those, the leader develops an individual coaching plan and, at the end, at the last one-on-one session, has either a modified plan or a new plan for going forward after the coaching is over. There's one other piece of the process, and that's the homework and the peer coaching. And really, just like one-on-one coaching where assignments might be there, there are some co-created agreements about what to practice or study or observe or notice or read. Each leader can expect to spend three hours every three weeks, in between the group sessions, reading, practicing, writing in a notebook, working with their peer coach—coaching their peer coach, actually—and pretty much participating in assignments relating to the group coaching.

KE: What kinds of organizations should consider group coaching, or when should an organization consider group coaching? Are there particular organizations that are more or less suited for it?

AD: I'm trying to think if there are organizations that I *don't* think could use group coaching! When they really are in a crisis and a time crunch is probably not the best time for coaching in general. Then, they might need a consultant in order to come to some decisions and a specific plan to execute. If there are actual crises they need to address as an organization, it is better to address those problems before initiating coaching.

Honestly, all kinds of organizations benefit from group coaching. I've done group coaching with technology organizations, as the one we depicted in this book. I have coached people from diverse organizations, who weren't all in the same company but came to the group from different places. It's amazing to me how common our challenges are, and the diversity we bring is partly in our individual perspectives and experiences. Group coaching works really well in all kinds of organizations and also across organizations.

KE: Anything to add, Holly?

HW: Typically, you are going to find more receptivity to it in organizations that really want to invest in people.

KE: Can you tell us a story from your experience of a situation where group coaching really did lead to the expansion of leadership capacity or substantive change for the organization and its leaders?

AD: The one that comes to mind is a group I did over six months' time with eight leaders. It was actually an interesting group in that there were two leaders each from four divisions in this company. They were all managers—and half were first-time managers. It was a pretty diverse group, mid-level in their place in the organization. The goal for the group was that they would become a team and bridge some of those silos that can happen across organizations. At the beginning, people only saw their own world and their own place in the organization. At the end they had a deep respect for their interdependence and how they all contributed to the organization's success. They got really good at challenging each other across silos, saying, "Hey, yes, you're doing that new product, but are you even thinking about the impact that's going to have on my team?" They learned to do that in a way that was not confrontational but was still challenging the other person to actually think bigger. At the end of the process, the relationships were

155

very, very different—and the results they were getting were also very different. They were getting results with less effort and more joy—even though they were challenging each other more. The results were better. Work seemed easier for the team and they were having more fun even though they were working just as hard.

KE: As I read the book and considered different situations, I wondered—how does the coach handle skeptics, those who might be a little suspicious of the group process?

HW: I typically employ a really great one-on-one session with each client as part of the design. People can express what they feel they need to express, including trepidations. In that first session, I am really exploring the questions, *"Are you coachable? Is this something you want to do?"* And I offer, *"Here, let me tell you a little about what it will be like, the structure and how things work."* So that when people come into that first group session, they are ready. Most of my clients don't make participation mandatory. The exception to that is team coaching. It's pretty hard to say you're not going to be part of the team. But for the group coaching, it's perceived as a great thing to be invested in and something people want to do. They are also given an option to opt out very early in the process when the commitment levels are described. Most of the time when that happens, it's explained to me that the choice is because of other work-related commitments or personal issues or something like that. But it could, in fact, be there are some skeptics that I never get to meet. I don't know. I find that first one-on-one conversation is a great place to start working on participation.

AD: One thing to add, Kate, is that people recognize: *I get to have my own goals for this experience. I get to customize this to be what I need as a leader and what I need for my own development. This experience is not somebody imposing their goals*

156

upon me. That's a gift, right? To have a structure of support to help you reach your goals. People realize pretty quickly with individual and group coaching: *Wow, even if somebody has recommended that I get a coach, when I actually enter coaching, I get to decide how I'm going to use this experience to be a better leader and maybe a better human being.*

HW: That's so great, Ann. Each leader in either sort of program—a group coaching program or team coaching—is really focused on *How can I be more effective as a leader* or *What's my current leadership capacity? Where can I stretch? What do I want for myself? How will that help my team?* And that's carried all the way through for each person.

KE: And there you have the benefit of individual coaching too, which is, *I can customize this to the need and concern I have right now.* It's not like training where we're teaching content to everybody, wanting them to come away with a body of knowledge that's quite well defined. This group coaching experience sounds more collaborative, between coach and group and also between individuals within the group.

HW: Definitely. And the accountability is sitting with the leaders to step into their own development. So coaches aren't "doing to" anybody; it's really a co-creation.

KE: You've written this book, and you're going to be helping both coaches and organizations understand their options with regards to group coaching. What do you really hope people will take away from reading the book?

AD: I guess what I hope coaches will take away is that group coaching isn't scary. The coaches who do group coaching find it amazingly fun, powerful, challenging, and inspiring. Many coaches steer away from group coaching because there are lots of things to track, lots of moving pieces, and competing agendas in some cases. However, I hope coaches will take away that group coaching is actually a true collaboration. You are co-creating a group experience with eight partners.

For leaders, I hope they will take away that *this has been an incredible way for me to develop myself and my relationships because I got to practice, and I also discovered my blind spots, things that I might not have brought to an individual coach because I didn't actually know my blind spots. I got to discover those thanks to the mirrors provided by others around me.*

For those in HR or OD functions, who are really responsible for developing their people in the organization, I hope what they'll discover is that group coaching is a great option for developing people. The book can help them understand what that might look like.

HW: I really think the book offers an opportunity for us coaches to reflect on what it's like to be a leader and being coached. I hope that the book gives a window into what happens when leaders are coached or opens up the imagination of the coach as to what can happen when leaders are coached in groups and in teams.

KE: You are pioneering the field of coaching with this introduction of group coaching and the distinctions you make between team coaching, group coaching, and individual coaching. Is there anything else you wanted to share?

AD: Two things for me, Kate. One of the things I'm noticing is that there have been five or six books now about group coaching, all written within the last four years. But they're all "about" group coaching. There are some great how-tos, processes, and structures, yet you don't get a good feel for what it would be like to be in the actual group sessions.

What we've tried to do with this book is give you a sense of what it is like to be in the room, whether you're a leader or a coach. What is that going to feel like?

The other thing we haven't touched on today is that our structure for group coaching includes introducing some tools, whether those are books that we think would be valuable or assessments. What you notice is that group coaching is not about training. We're not necessarily concerned about people mastering knowledge, rather we're offering a variety of tools and resources. Different individuals will really latch onto one tool that happens to be especially valuable to them. And then, part of what they do in group coaching is not only use the resource themselves; they also share its power with the rest of the group so that others will see opportunities to use that tool. This doesn't necessarily happen out of a training session or even one-on-one coaching.

KE: How did the two of you work together to create this book? It reads like one person wrote it.

HW: That's somewhat of a miracle, particularly since Ann and I don't even live in the same place and, in terms of really knowing each other well, we've learned about each other, and gotten to know each other, and become friends through the process of writing the book. I don't know how that happened. It's a co-creation, coaching miracle. I've just been very happy to have worked with Ann and be part of her unique background and large wisdom about what coaching is, and how it works, and how it works with people. So we just got really lucky, didn't we, Ann?

AD: I think we did. That was a big concern we had, Kate, whether we would have such different voices it would be hard to come up with one common voice. As it turned out, that part was easy and fluid. In a certain way, there's been a parallel process for us of learning from each other and being able to give each other feedback that's very much mirrored what happens for people in a group.

KE: You're right, it does read like one voice, and it's actually a wonderful piece of storytelling. I find the book very readable, and I can't wait to find out what happens next to the characters as I read it. I hadn't even thought about how two perspectives informed one narrative, and it's a book that really flows, tells a story, and does exactly what you said, Ann: brings us inside the group coaching process so that we'd actually know what it's like to participate in it.

If someone is reading the book and wants to try group coaching, how can they reach you?

HW: We have a website that's linked to the book called www.beingcoached. com. The website shares the stories in the book and some of the experiences that coaches have behind the scenes. Going to that website will be a great place to reach either or both of us and also follow some more stories about the coaching process.

KE: Anything else that would make this conversation complete for either of you?

AD: Just how much fun you are, Kate, and how cool it is to see you doing what you do. Thank you so much for doing this interview with us.

KE: I am honored and delighted to be a part of this process and to have the chance to feature you in this conversation. I really believe this book is a book that will potentially have the same kind of impact in the field of coaching as Lencioni did on the dysfunctions of the team, because you've translated these ideas into a fable that we can read, learn from, and enjoy. You've made it accessible to the reader as a concept, but also as a very readable learning story. Coaches and organizations owe you a big thank-you!

NOTES

1. TAIS Assessment, www.epstais.com.

2. Lazy Coaching Model, from a webinar by coach Michael Bungay
    Stanier, www.findyourgreatwork.com.

    In the coaching group, Jordan shares with participants the Lazy
    Coaching model for them to use in their peer coaching with one
    another, and on their work teams. The basic model is this:

    When someone comes to you with a problem, coach them to
    come up with their own solution. It's called Lazy Coaching because
    all you have to do is listen and ask questions; the other person does
    the work of finding their own solution. To use the Lazy Coaching
    method, notice when someone brings up a problem or has a
    complaint, and instead of giving advice or solving it for them, ask:

    -   What have you thought of?
    -   What else?
    -   What else?
    -   What else? (until they get an insight or reach an impasse)
    -   What's next?

3. David Rock, *Quiet Leadership: Six Steps to Transforming Performance at
    Work* (New York: HarperBusiness, 2007), 134–138.

4. TAIS Assessment, www.epstais.com.

5. Leadership coaches typically include an agreement about the confidentiality of client conversations. The International Coach Federation (ICF) Code of Ethics offers guidance to coaches that includes confidentiality of client information. (http://www.coachfederation.org/ethics)

6. Lazy Coaching is what Kim does in response to Sheila's complaint about her mother. Notice the positive results it has for Sheila, and the energy she experiences when she arrives at her own solution. By listening and asking Sheila questions, Kim enables Sheila to discover her own wisdom, and doing so energizes her to try out the solution she's created.

7. The Thinking Path is an approach to bring to our awareness the connection between our thoughts, emotions, actions, and results. Many great minds over the centuries (such as Epictetus and Kant) have made this connection with references to the thought-emotion-behavior connection. This connection is at the core of Cognitive-Behavioral Psychology. The Thinking Path tool has been popularized by Alexander Caillet. See his essay "The Thinking Path" in *On Becoming a Leadership Coach: a Holistic Approach to Coaching Excellence*, Christine Wahl, Clarice Scriber and Beth Bloomfield, eds. (New York: Palgrave Macmillan, 2008), 243–258.

8. Statistics from Cy Wakeman, *Reality-Based Leadership: Ditch the Drama, Restore Sanity to the Workplace, and Turn Excuses into Results* (San Francisco: Jossey-Bass, 2010). Lack of engagement at work has been well documented by Gallup, with a 71% figure of non-

engagement cited in their 2011 employee engagement survey. http://www.gallup.com/poll/150383/majority-american-workers-not-engaged-jobs.aspx

9.   Cy Wakeman, in *Reality-Based Leadership,* cites the 71% figure of workers who think about leaving their work on a regular basis, and believes that consistent, balanced feedback is one way to engage workers. The fictional webinar depicted here refers to Wakeman's approach to providing balanced feedback.

10.   Jordan has recommended several books as resources to the group participants. One is Susan Scott's *Fierce Conversations,* which offers tools to have more effective conversations that move a leader (or anyone) toward their goals and the quality relationships that will support them best. Susan Scott, *Fierce Conversations: Achieving Success at Work and in Life One Conversation at a Time* (New York: Berkley Trade, 2004).

11.   The National Speakers Association (NSA) is an organization for professional speakers. Since 1973, NSA has provided resources and education designed to advance the skills, integrity, and value of its members and the speaking profession. See more at: http://www.nsaspeaker.org/about/. Different chapters enable participants to practice their speaking and to get feedback in order to improve, which is what Raj is referring to here.

12.   *Quiet Leadership* is another of the books shared with group members. It provides a strong grounding in the neuroscience of how people work and lead. David Rock, *Quiet Leadership: Six Steps to Transforming Performance at Work* (New York: HarperBusiness, 2007).

13.   TED Talks is a daily video podcast of the best talks and performances from TED conferences, TEDx events, and partners—anywhere leading thinkers and doers give the talk of their lives in 18 minutes. See more at http://www.ted.com/pages/initiatives_tedtalks. Amy Cuddy, Harvard Social Psychology faculty member, did a popular TED talk in 2012, which at the time of writing this book had been seen by over 16 million viewers. Titled *Your Body Language Shapes Who You Are*, her talk described the research and results of how choosing different body postures can impact confidence and success in job interviews and other endeavors. To watch the talk Raj is referring to, go to http://www.ted.com/talks/amy_cuddy_your_body_language_shapes_who_you_are, filmed June 2012, accessed March 11, 2014.

14.   The Alexander Technique (www.amsatonline.org) and Feldenkrais Method (www.feldenkrais.com) are approaches to body movement which offer guidance and tools for awareness. Underlying each approach is the understanding that the postures we hold and the way we move our bodies also impact our brains, and the thoughts and emotions which arise. Raj is referring here to the many videos on YouTube which describe these techniques, which the reader may want to explore.

15.   The first element in Rock's "Think About Thinking" approach outlined in *Quiet Leadership* is enabling others to think for themselves. See pp. 35–44 especially, to dive deeper into Alice's approach here.

16. Sheila's comments on noticing refer to a tool that members have learned in their individual and group coaching: to notice what they are thinking, feeling, and doing without judgment. If they can consciously notice themselves, they can also choose to make changes. Without conscious awareness, changing our habits of thought and action is impossible.

17. Scott, *Fierce Conversations*, 7.

18. Ibid., 19–21.

19. Marianne is remembering the importance of how you begin a conversation, and recalling that Scott offers a great deal of guidance on opening statements. Ibid., 142–154.

20. Scott, *Fierce Conversations*, 91–123.

21. Ibid., 148–157.

22. The one-word check-in is a tool that group coaches often use to enable group members to become present in the group and to reflect on their own state of being. It is a valuable self-awareness tool as well as being useful for everyone in the group, including the coach, to have a sense of how the others are feeling. Many leaders report to us that it is a tool they adopt and use in many of their other workplace meetings. They find it serves the function of awareness, and also facilitates developing a more personal connection and sense of engagement. A short amount of time is taken for an approach that can have significant positive impact, whether in coaching or in other groups.

23. There are many resources that discuss the value of positivity in our lives and organizations. Barbara Frederickson's *Positivity* (Harmony, 2009) and Martin Seligman's *Authentic Happiness* (Atria Books, 2004) are two excellent resources. Raj is also talking here about the underlying neuroscience, and how we respond to one another at a brain level. Resources Raj and others might access to learn more include *Mirroring People: The Science of Empathy and How We Connect with Others,* by Marco Iacoboni (Picador, 2009) or the blog post "There's Magic in Your Smile," by Sarah Stevenson on *Psychology Today,* June 25, 2012, http://www.psychologytoday.com/blog/cutting-edge-leadership/201206/there-s-magic-in-your-smile, accessed March 11, 2014.

24. There are many resources that validate the notion that whatever we focus on, we get more of. One of our favorites is *The Power of TED**, an approach to enabling leaders and others to move from a focus on problems to a focus on desired outcomes. The result is a more sustained improvement than the up-and-down roller coaster of a problem focus. David Emerald, *The Power of TED* (The Empowerment Dynamic),* revised and updated (Bainbridge Island, WA: Polaris Publishing Group, 2009).

25. Scott, *Fierce Conversations,* front matter.

26. August Turak, "A Leadership Lesson from Meister Ekhart," *Forbes,* August 5, 2011, accessed March 11, 2014, http://www.forbes.com/sites/augustturak/2011/08/05/a-leadership-lesson-from-meister-eckhart/. See also August Turak's *Business Secrets of the Trappist Monks: One CEO's Quest for Meaning and Authenticity* (Columbia Business School Publishing, 2013).

27.   Nick Petrie, "Future Trends in Leadership Development," Center for Creative Leadership, December 2011, accessed March 11, 2014, http://www.ccl.org/leadership/pdf/research/futureTrends. pdf?campaign=HP0813

28.   The Deloitte Millennial Survey, January 2014. Accessed March 11, 2014, https://www.deloitte.com/assets/Dcom-Austria/Local%20 Assets/Documents/HCAS/Millenial%20Survey%202014.pdf

29.   Maria Konnikova, "Goodnight. Sleep Clean," *New York Times,* January 11, 2014, accessed March 11, 2014, http://www.nytimes. com/2014/01/12/opinion/sunday/goodnight-sleep-clean.html?_ r=0.

30.   Patrick M. Lencioni, *The Five Dysfunctions of a Team: A Leadership Fable* (San Francisco, CA: Jossey-Bass, 2002), 43, 187–190.

RESOURCES FOR COACHES, LEADERS, HUMAN RESOURCE PROFESSIONALS

COACHES

As a coach, you are accustomed to learning and reading books about coaching. Our hope is that as you read *Being Coached*, you didn't feel you were reading *about* coaching at all; rather, you experienced what it's like for leaders as they experience group coaching. And now that you've had that experience, we'd like to invite you to step out of the story, to gain perspective on what you just read, and to see ways you can apply it to your own coaching.

Taking a step back and reflecting on the leaders at Tech Environments and their experiences coaching, we'd like to ask you a few coaching questions so that you can create your own wisdom. As you read through the questions below, consider what you notice. How does this inform your own approach to group and team coaching? What other questions do you have?

The Coaching Program

- When a story engages you, it is easy to overlook details such as the underlying structure of the coaching program Jordan uses at Tech Environments. In thinking back about this structure, what elements do you notice?
- How does each component of the program—individual coaching sessions, group sessions, peer coaching, assessments, readings, tools, etc.—contribute to the development of individual leaders?

The Coaching Process

- How does the simple three-step approach of check-in, group dialogue, and check-out in the group coaching sessions contribute to group members' experience?
- What elements of Jordan's approach to group coaching are critical to establishing trust and a willingness to take risks?

The Coach's Approach

Jordan wants the leaders at Tech Environments to have skills in interacting with, challenging, and supporting one another that will last well beyond the time they are with her in the coaching program.

- What specific things did you notice Jordan doing in order to facilitate individual skills development and shared accountability?
- How does Jordan address issues of confidentiality in the group coaching? What is the impact of her approach for the leaders involved in these groups?
- How does Jordan's individually connecting with each group member before the group begins influence group coaching? Do you jump-start group coaching and the development of each participant with individual discovery sessions beforehand?

Group Membership

At the start of *Being Coached*, Director of Talent Management Patrick has a dilemma in retaining talent at Tech Environments. He's hoping that group coaching will be a solution and carefully selects the first group of leaders to pilot this approach. Patrick has some obvious candidates for the group—strong leaders who he believes could be even better, and for whom group coaching might add to their job satisfaction.

- What criteria are ideally used to select group participants? To what extent is a diverse group important to you, and to your client?
- What opportunities for "opting in" might exist that ensure the group consists only of those who want to be there? Would the group be strengthened if it also included reluctant participants?

Tools and Assessments

In addition to the coaching itself, Jordan provides additional tools for self-awareness and leadership effectiveness, including the TAIS assessment, David Rock's *Quiet Leadership*, and the Lazy Coaching model and Thinking Path tool.

- How can an individual assessment create greater self-awareness and engagement at the start of group coaching? What are the benefits of this approach? Is there any downside?
- What assessment, or kind of assessment, will you choose for the leaders you are serving?
- How did the different individuals in *Being Coached* access Jordan's recommended resources differently? How does this fit with the concept of honoring the client's agenda?
- What tools and resources will you share, or does that depend on what comes up within any given group?

Individual Versus Group Coaching

Individual coaching is more familiar to most coaches than group coaching, and more known to clients as well.

- What are the essential differences between individual and group coaching? When is one a better choice than the other?

- Recognizing that all the leaders in *Being Coached* did have some individual coaching sessions, do you believe any of them would have been better served by individual coaching alone?

Impact of Coaching

- In thinking about each of the characters in the book and the ways in which they developed, what changes did you notice in each one? How does the diversity of outcomes experienced validate the power of group coaching?
- Group and team coaching can change the fabric of a company as individual members act and interact differently. This can have a ripple effect in their teams. What are some of the secondary impacts you noted as you read *Being Coached*? Who else learned something new or changed their behavior in addition to those who were directly experiencing coaching?

Group Versus Team Coaching

We call it team coaching when an intact team shares a common goal in its members' daily work, as the C-suite leaders did in *Being Coached*. In team coaching, all group members share team goals as well as having their own individual development goals. In contrast, the mid-level leaders in *Being Coached* are not a team, even though they all work in the same organization.

- What other differences do you notice between the group coaching of mid-level leaders and the team coaching of those in the C-suite at Tech Environments? What similarities are there?
- How are groups different when the leaders come from eight different organizations instead of being in one company as they are in *Being Coached*? What value might group coaching offer in this circumstance?

Your Sweet Spot

As you read *Being Coached*, you likely enjoyed some leaders more than others. You probably also felt more at ease with some elements of Jordan's coaching approach than others.

- Noticing where you felt most engaged and excited as you read, what does this tell you about your ideal clients?
- Are there new tools or approaches that you could incorporate into your own coaching practice? What will you add that Jordan did not include?

LEADERS

As a leader, you may (or may not) be familiar with reading books about leadership and determining how to apply their lessons to your own experience. This section takes what happens in *Being Coached* and helps you apply it to your own development as a leader. Because we are coaches, we will mostly offer questions so that you can self-coach, or find a peer coach, or use the questions in a coaching engagement. Some of these suggestions will probably resonate with you and others will not, as they did for the characters in *Being Coached*. Please go to www.beingcoached.com for more about leaders self-coaching.

Self-Awareness

Self-awareness is at the foundation of leadership effectiveness. Becoming more conscious and aware of who you are in the moment and how you show up is essential for leaders who want to develop themselves. Greater self-awareness can come about by taking an assessment, by noticing what you are feeling emotionally and physically at a given moment, and by becoming more conscious of the ongoing stream of conversation you are having with yourself. Asking others how they experience you will also help build self-awareness. Each of these strategies is used in *Being Coached*, and each works for the different leaders depicted. Some options for you as a leader are:

- Take a self-assessment and a debrief coaching session to understand the results and make sense of them, given your specific role and your goals. Share the results with someone who knows you well and will support your taking action. What surprised you about your feedback?
- Notice and observe how you are feeling emotionally and physically in the moment. When stressed or distracted, ground your-

self by noticing the intake and exhalation of your breath as the characters in *Being Coached* do in order to pause. Use a notebook or online journal to keep track of your self-observations. What do you notice about your breath?

- Begin paying attention to your constant companion, your inner voice. What is the quality of the conversation you are having with yourself? Do you enjoy your constant companion? Is this inner voice overly critical? Are there other conversations you would rather have with yourself?

- Who could you ask for feedback on how you are showing up as a leader? (Be sure this is someone whose opinion you are interested in having, and whom you trust to have a positive intention.) Is there a 360-degree feedback assessment tool you could use where you work? Could your manager ask on your behalf?

If you already know what you'd like to work on, ask for Feed Forward, a methodology designed by Executive Coach Marshall Goldsmith to gather suggestions on how to improve one's performance (see Feed Forward at www.marshallgoldsmithlibrary.com). What surprised you about the feed forward you received?

Peer Coaching

Having a peer coach can help hold you accountable for your development. Peer coaches can be reading partners who share and discuss articles and books on leadership, and feedback providers to build self-awareness and choice in the moment. Try to think of someone trustworthy to share the inevitable triumphs and stumbles with.

- Who would be a good peer coach for you? Why? How can you describe the concept and value of peer coaching when you make your request?

Using a Coach Approach

Practicing using a coach approach with yourself (self-coaching), with your peer coach, and with your direct reports and peers can be a powerful leadership development strategy. The Lazy Coaching model developed by Michael Bungay Stanier and used by several characters in *Being Coached* helps leaders develop listening skills, engage others, and build leadership capacity for leading from the side and behind, rather than always from the front. The higher you go as a leader, the more you will depend on others' thinking and doing, so it is critical to understand how they think and to develop greater leadership capacity around you. Here is the Lazy Coaching model when someone brings you a problem:

- What have you thought of?
- What else?
- What else?
- What else? (until they get an insight or reach an impasse)
- What's next?

For you, the leader, the hardest part will be stopping yourself from automatically dispensing advice or an answer instead of taking a breath and choosing a coach approach.

Thinking Path

When breakdowns and dilemmas happen, the Thinking Path is a great model for leaders:

What am I THINKING? → What am I feeling? → How am I behaving? → What results am I getting? →

This model can be applied to describe what's going on in the present. It can also be used aspirationally—that is, what results would you like? How would you need to behave to get those, and what would you need to be thinking and feeling?

Other Resources

You may have found yourself responding positively to the "neuroscience as change management model" passages in *Being Coached*. Like Raj and Alice, some leaders really find neuroscience helpful in understanding how to change behavior. If this is true for you, or for your peer coach, there are many TED talks, articles, and books on neuroscience and behavior change. Where can you go to find more information on neuroscience?

Being Curious

Finally, leaders who want to develop their leadership capacity can remember to be curious. What is happening around you and inside you? Is there a way to engage more consciously in the moment? Manage distractions? Be more connected with others? What are you curious about? What would you like to learn about? Where can you just be and listen rather than directing and controlling? What would happen if you said nothing? Or if you spoke up when you are usually silent? Be curious! Take some risks to discover something you don't already know.

Check out the website www.beingcoached.com or additional tools and dialogue with other coaches, leaders, and human resource professionals.

HUMAN RESOURCE PROFESSIONALS

Human Resource professionals are often in the unenviable position of trying to meet all the talent recruitment and development needs of an organization. Depending on the company and its own stage of evolution, this demands a complex interplay of internal and external resources as well as attention to the organizational priorities, desired results, and the time and financial costs. Our hope is that reading *Being Coached* has enabled you to see this complex relationship of people, resources, and results clearly.

If you have an interest in bringing group or team coaching to your organization after reading *Being Coached*, we would like to offer you some suggestions based on our experience.

Value of Group and Team Coaching

First and foremost, it's important to be clear about why you are recommending group or team coaching (instead of, for example, leadership competency training).

If there is an appreciation for and understanding of the value of leadership coaching in your organization, your job is easier. If not, you will need to be able to distinguish why group coaching is the answer. Here are some questions:

- Are we developing leaders with a variety of individual leadership development goals?
- Would creating an ongoing learning community be helpful?
- Will allowing leaders a four- to six-month program with room for reflection and development build more leadership capacity?
- Do we want to shift our leadership culture?
- Will ensuring that accountability for development rests with the leader instead of a training program help us build leadership competencies?

Further, differentially investing in leaders in the middle of the organization needs to be well thought out and supported by performance management data or other considerations (diversity, for example):

- What criteria will we use to choose leaders for a group coaching?
- Would it make sense to consider a diverse pool of candidates?

It is also critical to have executive support or sponsorship for group coaching, and this support is the lifeblood of a team coaching program. If you are considering team coaching, you must be able to convince the team leader that she or he must be open to coaching and being coached. Jack, the CEO of Tech Environments in *Being Coached*, is a typical leader. He starts the team coaching thinking that others need to get along better, but it doesn't take long for him to realize that he is part of the problem—both in how he leads the team and how he interacts with others. A team leader who is unwilling to be transparent can doom a team coaching engagement.

- How much is coaching understood and used in my organization?
- Do leaders understand that coaching is a "good to great" play, rather than being used for remediation of problem behaviors?
- Does the senior executive team believe in coaching?
- Do leaders understand that accountability for development rests with them?
- Will the leader of an intact team be willing to be coached in a team coaching program?

Administrative Work Required for Group and Team Coaching

In addition to sponsorship and willingness to be coached, bringing in group and team coaching requires some additional administrative work to calendar leaders, bring in assessments and other resources, and make space

179

for their participation, including homework between sessions. The coach will also need support for booking rooms and making sure there is time and space for one-on-one coaching. Questions to consider:

- Do we have the administrative support we need to schedule leaders and conference rooms for multiple sessions, including one-on-one coaching?
- Will we be able to support the coach in assessment-taking and other resourcing processes?

Evaluation of the Effectiveness of Group and Team Coaching

It is critical to develop a robust evaluation process for group and team coaching. Evaluation should include feedback from the manager of the participant, and ideally would take place again, six months after the group or team coaching program concludes. If possible, going beyond the Kirkpatrick level 1 evaluation questions will provide the best data on effectiveness. The application of what leaders experience in group and team coaching is the largest win for the organization. Please go to www.beingcoached.com for sample level 2 and 3 evaluation questions.

Please contact us if you would have additional questions or comments. Check out the website www.beingcoached.com for additional tools and dialogue with other coaches, leaders, and human resource professionals.

Made in the USA
Middletown, DE
18 June 2016